BY THE THREE GREAT ROADS

D1387316

BY
THE THREE
GREAT ROADS

· A History of Tollcross ·
· Fountainbridge and the West Port ·

EDITED BY DREW EASTON

AUP

First published in 1988
Aberdeen University Press
A member of the Pergamon Group

© Tollcross Local History Project 1988

British Library Cataloguing in Publication Data

By the three great roads: a history of
   Tollcross, Fountainbridge and the West Port
   1. Edinburgh. Tollcross, history
   I. Tollcross Local History Project
   II. Easton, Drew
   941.3′4

ISBN 0 08 036587 6

Printed in Great Britain
The University Press
Aberdeen

Contents

List of Illustrations

Cover illustration: The Old Snooker Hall
(*Painting reproduced by permission of the artist, George Brown*)

All illustrations reproduced by courtesy of Edinburgh City Libraries were photographed by Peter Ross

Acknowledgements

Many thanks are due to past members of the project: Chris Ritchie, Rachel Greer, May Scott, Rob Burns, Willie Campbell, Ian Christie, Thelma Harris, Toby Porter and Wilfred Grubb. Research for the oral history was carried out by Ruth McLennan in conversation with Mrs M Main, Mrs M Grubb, Mr D Anderson, Mr D Pinkerton and Mr J McKenzie, with additional material by Catherine Toall and Jean Redgers; our thanks to them. Support for the project was gratefully received from staff of the Community Education Service under the auspices of Lothian Regional Council and also to the Management Committee of Tollcross Community Centre. Our thanks are also due to Hilary Kirkland of the Scottish Local History Forum and to Malcolm Cant for their encouragement and advice. We were pleased to have benefited from the help of Mr Bathgate, Mr Fraser, Mrs McLennan, Father Giblin, John Dames, the Reverend Michael Hill, Helen Rowbotham, volunteers at St Cuthbert's Church, Stuart Harris, Professor A J Aitken, Norma Armstrong, Sheena McDougall, Charles McMaster, Derek Adams, George McMillan, Dr Meechie, Betty McAnna, Arnott Wilson and many others.

Our research would have been impossible without the patient and helpful assistance from the staff of the following organisations: The Edinburgh Room and the Scottish Section of Edinburgh Central Public Library, The Scottish Records Office, New Register House, The National Monuments Record of Scotland, The Public Records Office in Kew, The National Library of Scotland, Huntly House Museum, Edinburgh District Council Archives, Heriot-Watt Brewing Archives, Lothian Health Board Archives, University of Edinburgh (Department of Community Medicine), Scotmid Ltd, Distillers PLC, the Master Bakers Association.

Very special thanks are due to Rachel Greer and Sharon Fowler for their patience and hard work typing the drafts, and to Sharon Fowler for painstakingly going over the whole text for corrections several times over! Thank you to Aberdeen University Press for making it all possible.

Last, but not least, a personal thanks from the Editor to June Simpson (Tollcross born and bred) for her emotional support throughout the project.

Here's to the people of Tollcross, Fountainbridge and the West Port, past and present!

List of Contributors

George Brown was raised in Fountainbridge, is self-employed as an artist having graduated in History from the University of Stirling. He is also a time-served painter and decorator.

Jane Curr was brought up in Juniper Green and is a graduate in Law from the University of Aberdeen. She is Deputy Editor of the *Tollcross Times*.

Drew Easton, born in Leicester has been in Edinburgh since childhood. He graduated in Psychology from the University of Stirling and is now employed as a Community Education Worker at Tollcross Community Centre.

Mary MacDonald, a native of Birkenhead has lived in Edinburgh for the past forty-nine years. Before her retirement she was an Assistant Secretary in the Scottish Office.

Jean Redgers, now retired, spent her childhood in the vicinity of Tollcross. After many years in the south of England she returned and worked with the mentally handicapped at Gogarburn Hospital in Edinburgh.

Catherine Toall was brought up in Dundee Place. Prior to retirement she worked as a Clerical Officer at the Royal Victoria Dispensary in Spittal Street.

1

The Origins Of Tollcross

Drew Easton

Introduction

Tollcross of today is not all it appears to be. Any notion that it is so-named because of the familiar 'spokes of a wheel' crossroads is, for the most part, unfounded. The earliest road to join the ancient road south from the Old Town of Edinburgh—now the High Riggs and Home Street—was Lothian Road, built in the 1780s. The name Tollcross appears much earlier than this and there is no evidence of a Toll ever having been situated at this point.

The earliest reference to a Tollcross was in 1439. It is much more likely that this was to be found at the head of modern day West Port at the crossroads leading north, west and south. The later Lands of Tollcross were named after this ancient Toll and continued to be so referred at least until the late nineteenth century.

This chapter describes the Lands of Tollcross and those which surround it. These lands were anciently parts of the Royal Orchards, from the reign of David I, and their rural nature persisted until the eighteenth century when they were consistently sub-divided and held by the growing merchant classes who were leaving the Old Town in favour of country houses and the New Town.

During the nineteenth century, as Tollcross and district continued to grow in population, the residential attractions decreased. The exodus of the merchant classes was hastened by the growth of Industry which in turn was influenced by growing road communications in the area, and later canal and railway networks. All but one of these mansion residences have disappeared.

As the population grew and new streets were built we see the first indication of the name Tollcross, formerly referring only to the lands, now describing a succession of streets along the whole length of its eastern border. It is more than likely that the local landlord had an influence in naming these streets and in so doing he helped to compound the name in the general area of Tollcross which, by the end of the nineteenth century, had become one of Edinburgh's most famous crossroads.

While the exact origin and function of the nineteenth century Tollcross is unclear the development of the name provides the basis of this first chapter, with a brief description of the area's history over the intervening centuries.

Grass Roots

The origins and history of Tollcross and district begins in the mid twelfth century in the reign of David I (1124–1153), although the derivation of the name Tollcross still remains somewhat obscure. While the earliest discovered documentation of the name does not appear until 1439 it is possible to imagine what the general area of Tollcross was like in mediaeval times and to see how place names and even the very physical shape of the area has survived the intervening ages.

Tollcross of today and the lands which surround it were at this time part of the Barony of Inverleith, held in sergeanty by successive important people in the King's personal duty. During the reign of William I (1165–1214) it was held by his Baker and, in the reign of Alexander III (1249–1286) it was held by Sir William de St Clare, a distinguished knight, Sheriff of Edinburgh, and Keeper of the Royal Pantry. From 1350 these lands were held by successive members of the Touris or Towers family for the next three hundred years.

The Towers family came into possession of the lands of Orchardfield, Tollcross, Dalry, Pocketslieve and High Riggs (to be described later) as a gift from David II to Walter Towers, an Edinburgh merchant of French heritage. By the mid seventeenth century the lands were owned by the last remaining member of the family, Jean Towers, who married Sir John Sinclair of Long-formacus.

Fig 1.1: King's Stables Road taken from the Castle showing the main Tilting Ground, the shape of which still remains from the fourteenth century.

Between the twelfth and fifteenth centuries the area around the Castle to the west and south, which today corresponds to the bounds of the West Port, King's Stables Road, the West End of Princes Street, Haymarket and Morrison Street, were orchardlands (market gardens) belonging to the Crown and kept by serfs. The extent of these orchards varied over the centuries and may even have gone further south and east to the lands of Tollcross and High Riggs, whose borders were the Burgh Muir on the south and Potterrow on the east. However, the most important area of these Gardens of the Castle were around King's Stables Road, Lothian Road and the stretch of land once occupied by the Caledonian station and goods yard.

In the Royal Orchards were grown a wide variety of vegetables (onions, leeks, syboes, cabbages, peas, beans and garlic) which were marketed near to the King's Stables, immediately outwith the Grassmarket. Fruits such as apples, pears, cherries, strawberries and plums were in abundance as well as flowers and herbs grown for culinary and medicinal purposes—roses, gilliflowers, cinnamon flowers, crocuses and primroses. Apart from the cultivation and marketing of these products, the Royal Gardens were also a place of relaxation and entertainment, a place where people would sing and dance during the summer months and guests of the Castle would be entertained amidst the colourful admixture of flowers, fruits, fish ponds and rabbit warrens.

Less idyllic, but perhaps more exciting, were the displays of tilting (mediaeval jousting) which took place on the Barras (or Barrace), a grassed area on the south side of King's Stables Road between the Grassmarket and (including) the modern car park site. During his occupation of the Castle between 1335 and 1341 Edward III planned out and started to build the King's Stables and Tournament ground. After he was expelled, David II finished the work, being a collector of fine horses and who, in this age of chivalry and brutality, was a lover of Knightly Tournaments.

Standing in the castle today it is easy to imagine how Royalty of the time would view this spectacle in comfort. From there one can still see the shape of part of the Barras in the form of the District Council Cleansing Department and Regional Council Roads Department building which around the turn of the century was a Police Yard and Stables. Between the fifteenth and nineteenth centuries maps of the area show that the grassed area remained intact, perhaps used for grazing, but by 1800 the easterly portion described above became a slaughterhouse (the Shambles) and the westerly side was a small community called Livingston's Yards, both owned by George Combe, Brewer.

At a further distance, on the lands of Dalry, bordering those of Orchardfield (as they were later known) and Tollcross, there was also extensive cultivation of grain crops. The name Dalry, which means King's Farm or Fields, has roots in Celtic times but has survived into modern days. Closer to Tollcross a small hamlet on the eastern corner (and opposite) Semple Street and Morrison Street called Castlebarns grew during these times, housing labourers and farmworkers from the Dalry estate. Both Castlebarns and the King's Stables had granaries connected to them.

By 1500 the Gardens had fallen into great disrepair, not least because of invasion from the south which, for example, in 1335, after plunder by the English Army, left the gardens completely ruined. While the gardens did survive, the Castle, as far as a favoured place of residence for subsequent Kings was concerned, did not. Consequently the lands were leased to private market gardeners, possibly former serfs, who were empowered by their

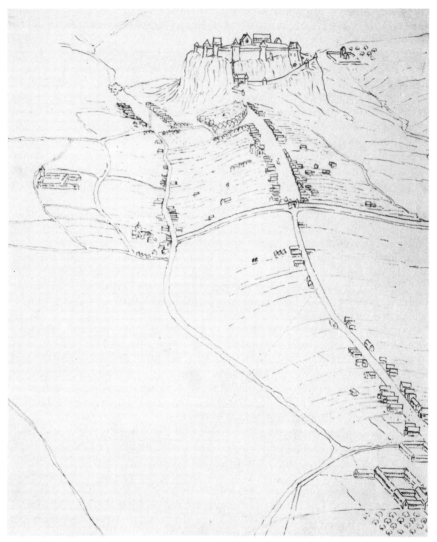

Fig 1.2: Edinburgh c 1450 showing the main route to the town by way of Newbigging (the Grassmarket) and the West Bow, and the arterial roads of Tollcross leading north, west and south.

superiors to maintain good standards of cultivation, or risk fines or imprisonment.

It is fair to assume that the area we call Tollcross today had an early association with the Royal Gardens and would have been taken over by private market gardeners. Although there is no direct evidence of this, it is interesting to note that the then Royal Orchards became the lands of Orchardfield, whose name survived well into the nineteenth century in the form of the street name Orchardfield, now Bread Street. On a map of 1881 the short section of modern Bread Street between Spittal Street and the West Port was called Orchardfield Street.

Bread Street marked the northern boundary of the lands of Tollcross and even as late as 1788 a sasine describing the erection of a tenement on these lands refers to the 'Garden of Tollcross', part of which was owned by a James Weir, architect, whose father James Weir, earlier in the century, is described as a 'Gardener in Tollcross'. In the nearby area of Heriot's Work, now the grounds of Heriot's School, was to be found a John Weir, gardener around 1722, who was also a founder member of the Society and Fraternity of Gardeners in the Shire of Midlothian formed in that year. Although many of the members of this Society were not gardeners, at this time the economic value of market gardening was recognised and the Society became wealthy enough to have erected in Gardner's Crescent (named after William Gardner WS a century later) a large house called Gardeners' Hall on the site of the modern crescent.

Other parts of Tollcross and district also developed their gardening heritage. The north croft of Tollcross was described in 1728 as 'fruit yards' and by 1782 the same area was a 'nursery garden' owned by James Richmond. Further west in Fountainbridge was a large Nursery Garden owned by James Gordon, who in 1758 published a *Catalogue of Shrubs and Flowers* which contained no less than 500 varieties of shrubs, trees, plants and seeds. Before listing each one James Gordon states:

> In this list are many curious plants, not to be found in any collection for sale in Scotland, and it is proposed to augment the Collection with as many foreign plants as can be naturalised to this Climate.
>
> At the same place may be had American Ever-greens and Deciduous Trees and Shrubs, with the best kinds of Fruit and Barren Nursery.
>
> Likewise Kitchen-garden, Grass and Tree Seeds, with Asparagus, Artichoaks, Strawberry, Sellery, Coliflower, Brocoli and Cabbage Plants; all at most reasonable Rates.

Crow's feet

The distinctive rural nature of Tollcross district remained until the eighteenth century, disturbed only by further invasion from the south, graphic illustration of which can be seen from a 'Facsimile of a plan of the Siege of the Castle of Edinburgh, May 1573', showing English soldiers encamped and attacking from positions to the south west and west of the Castle, in the area

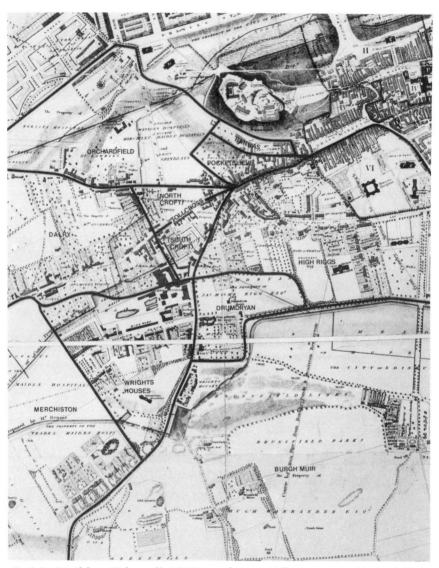

Fig 1.3: Detail from Kirkwood's 1817 map showing Tollcross area and beyond. Upon it is a tracing which shows the lands of Dalry, Orchardfield, Polcatslieve, High Riggs, the north and south crofts of Tollcross, Drumdryan, Valleyfield, Wright's Houses, as well as the Barras and the Burgh Muir.

we now call Lauriston, Tollcross, Lothian Road and West Princes Street Gardens. St Cuthbert's Church can be seen surrounded by embattlements and cannons.

Of particular interest in this facsimile is the road we now call West Port, leading to the 'crow's feet' shape of the routes to the north, west and south, which nowadays are called Bread Street, East Fountainbridge and High Riggs. In an earlier drawing of Edinburgh (c 1450), the significance of these roads is more clear, especially the road to the north, which is seen trailing away to the River Forth at Stirling, then the only land route to the north of Scotland. The other roads led respectively to Glasgow and Carlisle.

The shape of these roads and the lands surrounding Tollcross remain until today and help us to understand the position of the lands of Tollcross, which are not referred to until the seventeenth century.

The first available reference to Tollcross appears in a Royal Charter granted in 1439 by a John Touris (or Towers) to his son Peter for the sale of the bordering lands of High Riggs. John Touris is described as the Laird of Dalry, the lands of which are referred to earlier as also bordering Tollcross. The lands of the High Riggs may have been in the hands of the Touris family as early as 1350, in the shape of Sir John de Touris, who was one of David II's foremost knights, and they were held by that family at least until 1648.

Within this Charter, which the King confirmed in 1458, reference is made to 'the Tolcors' as being the westerly point of the lands of High Riggs, by the King's highway, leading from the town of Edinburgh, which today is called the West Port. Because this charter refers to 'the Tolcors' rather than the lands of Tollcross suggests that it is a point of reference—of whatever function—after which the lands were named.

'Tollcross' has been written variously over the centuries, from the above 'Tolcors' to 'Tollcroce', 'Towcorse', 'Towcroce' and even 'Tolcrow'! Even as late as 1787, in a sasine describing the sale of a piece of ground for the purpose of building, we find the area described as a 'part of Towcorse or Tollcross'.

To many people the word Tollcross suggests a point at which one crosses over a toll point, to pay dues for the upkeep of a road. It also has connotations of a crossroads. In fact there is no evidence of a toll ever having been in the position we call Tollcross today and, in the fifteenth century, the only crossroads in the vicinity are those mentioned above, at the top of the West Port, called the Two-penny Custom in the eighteenth century and the Main Point in the nineteenth and twentieth centuries—where the modern day 'Burke and Hare' public house now stands.

The importance of these crossroads cannot be understated and it seems reasonable to suppose that this was the position of the Tollcross five centuries ago. Dunlop, in her book *Anent Old Edinburgh* describes the Main Point in typical Victorian elegance:

> By the three great roads indicated, all that pertained to victory or defeat; all that belonged to commerce, to trade, to manufactures; all that had interest with agriculture, and with such as have cattle, and the hired labourers connected with both; all the prosperity, the industry, and the godliness; all the beggary,

the want, and the crime took the Main Point on the right and left shoulder, passed down the main street of Portsburgh, and entered the city by the West Port.

Before the West Port was built in the sixteenth century which, apart from its purposes of defence, functioned as a Toll point, what better place to exact dues than at this point of convergence of three of the most important trade routes to the town. Almost certainly it was the site of a Tolbooth after the Two-penny Custom was introduced in 1680 on every pint of ale and drinking beer, brewed, sold, or consumed in the Town and outlying territories. A Tollbooth was situated on the west corner of Lady Lawson Street and the West Port (now a Post Office building) and was later described as the Manse, or Sclate Barn. The custom was intended to raise funds for a Register House (over £4000 a year by the mid eighteenth century) from various points around the City. In spite of this tax the West Port, Tollcross and Fountainbridge became major brewing areas of Edinburgh.

The only other Toll point known in the area was Wright's Houses' Toll on modern day Leven Street opposite the appropriately named Old Toll Bar. Often referred to as the 'Toll-Cross', Wright's Houses' Toll was introduced in accordance with the 1755 Turnpike Act for the purposes of road repairs and development. At this time the village of Wright's Houses, the first building of which was erected in 1713, was on both sides of modern day Barclay and Bruntsfield Place, and the road was narrow and in a bad state of upkeep. In 1792 the westerly half was demolished and the road widened to sixty feet but the toll charge, still in effect, became an ever increasing source of annoyance to the increasing population of Bruntsfield and Morningside who travelled to and from the City. Not only had they to pay two pence to pass the toll point but also were often charged higher prices than normal for goods which were subject to the one shilling toll charge, by some merchants who used this as an excuse to recoup this sum from every customer. In 1852 Sir John Stuart Forbes, who owned the feu on whose lands the toll stood, attended a Public Meeting speaking in favour of the removal of the toll. To the relief of all concerned the Road Trustees agreed to its removal to the foot of Morningside Road two years later and which remained there until the repeal of the Turnpike Act in 1883.

Although no direct evidence has been found which links the fifteenth century Tollcross with the Main Point it seems likely that this is a more probable site. The purpose of the toll can be described from a lecture on Mediaeval Edinburgh by C A Malcolm in 1937 in which he mentioned:

> The important part played by immigrants from Flanders, England and other Scots Burghs in Mediaeval times in the evolution of markets from those around St Giles to the great markets that extended to the full extent of the late fifteenth century burgh. Tollcross, Cameron and Bonnington had toll booths, where dues were paid on all livestock taken to market.

Colonisation

Between 1760 and 1827 the population of Edinburgh doubled, rising from 60 000 to 120 000 people. This remarkable increase in such a short space of time is mirrored in the development of Tollcross and district, especially in the first quarter of the nineteenth century.

During the eighteenth century however we find Tollcross and district a residential alternative to the Old Town, now overcrowded and crumbling. While many of the growing middle classes moved to the New Town, there were significant numbers of mansions, great and small, in the Tollcross area. By the middle of the nineteenth century many of these mansions had disappeared, eclipsed by new housing programmes. Tollcross by the nineteenth century had also become an important communications point between the New Town and the Old, by way of Lothian Road in the 1780s, before the South Bridge was built in 1827. Also, during the period between 1820 and 1850 the Union Canal and the Caledonian Railway company had forged their way into the heart of the area. So too had industry begun to encroach on this previously rural land: Lochrin Distillery, Drumdryan Brewery, Gilmore's Rope Works, McEwan's Brewery and the Meat Industries, steadily transformed the area. Eventually little must have appealed to those who could afford to live in the mansions described below. Only a few of the many mansions are given here.

Wright's Houses
One of the oldest mansions in the area was the ancient Baronial home of William Napier, a branch of the Merchiston family whose lands adjoined those of Wrychtis Housis. Variously known as Bruntsfield Castle, Burghmuir Castle and Barganie House (after its occupant in 1791) it was probably built around 1339. It is described in 1785 as for sale, comprising:

> a court and two gardens, south and north, with a small dwelling house. Two parks or enclosures called Back Park to the west and south of the mansion and Lady's Acre to the east. The subjects are exceedingly convenient by the new Lothian Road.

Within fifteen years of this advertisement the Mansion was demolished, hardly without public comment, to make way for Gillespie's Hospital.

The origin of the name Wrychtis Housis is somewhat obscure but may refer to the Laird of Wright. What 'Wright' was, is not known. However, there are many remains of the mansion still in existence, dating back to the fourteenth century. Several sculptured stones and a sundial have been identified in the Lothians and Fife. For example within the stone wall of the garden of a mansion owned by the Admiralty in St Margaret's near North Queensferry, can be seen two stones with the Napier crest and initials. Likewise in a garden wall of the old mansion of Woodhouselee on the Biggar Road near Penicuik, long since demolished, there are several stones. The whereabouts of the sundial, which was most certainly in the grounds of Woodhouselee, is now unknown. The earliest surviving stone, dated 1376,

Fig 1.4: A drawing of Wrychtis Housis (Wright's Houses) (front view) showing the heraldic pediments above the windows dating from the fourteenth century.

is an heraldic pediment with the initials WN and JF, signifying the marriage between William Napier and Janet Forrester.

The site of the mansion of Wrychtis Housis is now occupied by a Sheltered Housing complex for the elderly, opposite Gillespie Crescent.

Dalry and Fountainbridge
Dalry House, which still stands today in Orwell Place (off Dalry Road) was built in the mid seventeenth century by Bailie Walter Chieslie, and was sold to Sir Alexander Brand in 1696, who later changed its name to Brandsfield House. Several streets built in the eighteenth and nineteenth centuries were named after Brandfield, the only surviving one being Brandfield Street at the top of Grove Street.

The Lands of Dalry or Brandfield stretched from Henderson Terrace, along Fountainbridge (approximately) to Semple Street, and bordered by Morrison Street to Haymarket and the whole length of Dalry Road.

Brand himself was notable in public life at the turn of the seventeenth century, a shrewd business man associated with the Merchant Company. Unfortunately his many business ventures got the better of him and by 1706 he was virtually bankrupt. By 1714 he had sold Brandsfield House although he retained much of the lands to the east around Fountainbridge, which passed down to his son, Alexander.

The Brands were responsible for developing their lands for both residential and commercial purposes. Several mansions were built in the area, notably Bainfield, Gardeners' Hall and Fountain House. Two brewers from Portsburgh, Bailie Robert Mitchell and Thomas Hodge, were among the first to move to what for many years was a secluded residential area for the middle classes and aristocracy. It is widely believed that the name Fountainbridge was adopted by the Brands, in place of the former Foullbridge, referring to the bridge over the foul waters of the Dalry Burn, in order that the property would sound more attractive.

Lauriston

The mansions of Lauriston were built on the lands of High Riggs, which were fields on the high ridge of land bordered by the Borough Loch (now the Meadows) to the south, and the town of Wester Portsburgh (West Port) on the north. They stretched from Potterrow on the east to modern day Tollcross on the west.

Several mansions with extensive grounds were built along the elevated ground above the loch and, during the eighteenth century, owned, for example, by the Hogs of Newliston (site of the Lothian Health Board building at the corner of Lauriston Place and Lauriston Park), the Earl of Wemyss (site of Chalmers Hospital) and William Borthwick of Crookston, whose house built in 1770 still stands to this day, occupied by St Catherine's Convent, at the corner of Lauriston Place and Gardens. In 1850 it was known as Lauriston Lodge.

Situated opposite Lord Wemyss' property was the three storey high Ramsay Lodge, at the corner of Lady Lawson Street, where now stands the Art College and the Old Fire Station. Further west in Lauriston Street was a large mansion where the Sacred Heart Church can now be found and can be seen clearly on the drawing illustrated in this Chapter entitled Tollcross around 1780.

Further north at the eastern corner of Lauriston Street and West Port was the mansion called High Riggs which, according to Dunlop had a feu charter connected with it of 1564 and which was extensively rebuilt until its demolition in 1877. A drawing of this house can be seen in Grant's *Old and New Edinburgh* (Lauriston Street side) and is evident on an improvement plan of 1791.

Lochrin

The lands of Drumdryan (Celtic name signifying a Blackthorn Ridge) stretch from Wright's Houses, along Leven and Home Streets to Tollcross, and are bounded on east by the Meadows. In the 1730s a Patrick McDowall built a Mansion called Drumdryan House on the site of the Kings Theatre, which was renamed Leven Lodge in 1750 when it was purchased by Alexander, fifth Earl of Leven—hence the street name, Leven Street. Leven Lodge was demolished in 1905 to make way for the King's Theatre which opened in 1906.

By 1788 the lands of Drumdryan were owned by James Home Rigg of Morton and Downfield, near Cupar, Fife, whose family lived in Tarvit House, south of Cupar. The mansion he occupied was built in 1774 and this was also named Drumdryan House. It was situated in what is now the back greens of the tenements of Drumdryan Street, Tarvit Street and Brougham Place, and, latterly, was accessible through a pend, still in existence in Tarvit Street, which now leads to an electricity sub-station. The house was demolished in 1958. The Home Rigg family moved from this house in 1794 but were responsible for the building of tenements, built around 1820 from the foot of

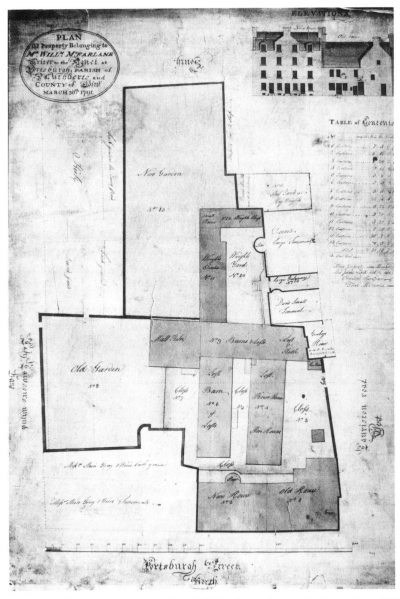

Fig 1.5: The above improvement plan of 1791 shows the ancient mansion of High Riggs built in 1563.

Lauriston Place over Brougham Street to Tarvit Street, and owned them until the 1850s.

Further south, Valleyfield House built in the mid seventeenth century, was demolished in the early nineteenth century to make way for housing in Glengyle Terrace (1869).

Across from Leven Lodge was Lochrin House, or Park House, which was actually on the lands of Wright's Houses. It was built by Samuel Gilmore in the mid eighteenth century, whose Rope Works were along the north side of Gilmore Place, backing onto the Union Canal. It was possessed by James Haig of Lochrin Distillery in 1797. In 1799 the house appears on the market, described as:

> That neat and commodious house on the Lothian Road near the Wright's Houses Toll, presently possessed by James Haig and lately painted, consisting of 11 fire rooms, 3 of which are 23 feet by 16 feet—with two neat Lodges in front—a grass park may also be had if required, also two other neat lodgings of two stories each, a little to the west on a new line of road (to become Gilmore Place). Apply to Samuel Gilmore, ropemaker there.

Lothian Road
Lothian Road runs through the lands of Orchardfield described earlier. Further to the east, between the King's Stables Road and the West Port also lies the lands of Pocketslieve or Polcatslive of which little is known. The lands were also known as Elvanside, which refers to the star constellation Orion, the Hunter, six stars of which can be seen on the crest belonging to the Towers family of Inverleith, who owned the land. It is possible that Polcatslive referred to the animal the Polecat, which was popular for its skin from mediaeval times until the eighteenth century when they became scarce and eventually died out in lowland Scotland. In 1619 a William and Thomas Weir are described as living in the 'tail' of Pocketslieve, presumably the narrowing section of the land behind Wester Portsburgh. It is likely that a large house, garden and well depicted on the seventeenth century map 'A Birds Eye View' (see Chapter 2) belonged to William Towries of Elvanside in 1530, 'Superior of the land beyond the West Port'.

Other notable houses in the eighteenth and nineteenth centuries were Maryfield, which stood opposite St Cuthbert's Church on King's Stables Road, and Kirk Brae House which stood on the site of the Caledonian Hotel. Kirk Brae was described by James Grant as an eighteenth century country villa of three stories, tall and narrow, occupied by the then Lieutenant General of the Castle, Lord John Elphinstone. Before being demolished in the mid nineteenth century to accommodate the extensions of the Caledonian Railway company, it was occupied by a skilled tradesman who held the position of 'The King's Carpenter for Scotland'.

Tollcross
The lands of Tollcross constituted around nine or ten acres bounded by Bread Street/Morrison Street, Semple Street/Thornybauk, and Home Street/High Riggs. By 1662 the lands were referred to as the north and south crofts, both

of equal acreage, split by Fountainbridge and East Fountainbridge. Ownership of these lands over the centuries is complex but the known land owners and proprietors are listed in Appendix I.

Only one mansion on these lands is worthy of note, the mansion of Tollcross which was situated near the corner of Bread Street and East Fountainbridge, built by a Patrick Browne between 1654 and 1662. Unfortunately nothing else is known about this mansion so far. However, that it was situated so close to the Main Point adds weight to the suggestion that the Tollcross was at that position.

One other building, however, does have great significance in Tollcross, that which was, along with the south croft of the lands of Tollcross, owned by the Weir family already mentioned above. The house was situated between Riego and Earl Grey Street and the foot of the High Riggs where now stands the Department of Employment Building, soon to be demolished and relocated. The house remained intact until the 1850s and in the 1851 Census a large house, converted into three small units, referred to as Tollcross Hall, may have been the Weir's house.

It is unlikely that the above mentioned James Weir, Gardener in Tollcross, owned this particular house, but it is known that his son James Weir, Architect, did and may well have built it. He is known to have built at least one other house in the area and, incidentally, was contracted in 1773 'to complete the structure of St Cuthbert's Church on foundations already laid' (that is the previous structure to the modern church). It is known that he designed the preaching box and the two-tier balcony. He died of 'fever' in 1779 at the age of fifty-three and was buried, strangely enough, in an unmarked grave in Rannie's tomb (a near neighbour in Portsburgh) in St Cuthbert's Churchyard.

His eldest son, also James, inherited both the house at Tollcross and the south croft of Tollcross, and it is he who was responsible for much of the building development in Tollcross at the turn of the nineteenth century, greatly influenced by the new Lothian Road in the 1780s, the south end of which passed through his property.

This James Weir was appointed as a Lieutenant in the (Royal) Marines prior to 1795 when he was promoted to Captain, and to Major in 1799. Although he was due to retire in 1802 it is known that in 1801 and 1805 he was sent to Malta with his company of the Maltese Light Battalion, serving under Brigadier General and later Colonel Thomas Graham, who became Lord Lyndoch. His duties were to recruit men 'towards completing the Detachments of His Majesties Ships in the Mediterranean, and sending surplus to England (if any), towards completing the Corps to its Establishment'. Presumably the Marines suffered heavy losses during the Peninsular War.

Major Weir and his family purchased and moved to Old Drumsheugh House around 1800 (described as 6 Lyndoch Place but not the terraced houses built in 1820 and still standing), half of which his father had bought in 1776. Major Weir had two sons; Thomas Graham Weir, MD (possibly named after Colonel Thomas Graham, Lord Lyndoch), and James Weir, MD.

The Major passed away in 1820 and his surviving wife Jean Stuart Ponton carried on the family interest in Tollcross until her death in 1848. James died in 1842 without issue and therefore all the family wealth passed to T Graham Weir.

T Graham Weir was born in 1812, attended Edinburgh Academy and married Margaret Lumsdaine. He was one of the original medical staff of the Royal Hospital for Sick Children, where he was Consultant Physician until he was seventy-six years old. He died in 1896 leaving a daughter, Isabella, and her husband, Archibald Inglis, MD. Their children Jane Stuart, Jessie Spens, Margaret Graham and Henry Alves Inglis, inherited the interests in Tollcross on their grandfather's death and, at the time, were known to be living in his house at 36 Heriot Row.

As will be seen in the next section, the influence of the Weirs in the development of the name Tollcross becomes apparent. A list of those people with the family name of Weir can be seen in Appendix II.

Consolidation

Tollcross as a place name has survived for 500 years but the crossroads we call Tollcross today may only have a history going back 100 years. While the

Fig 1.6: Viewed from Lochrin above the Dalry Burn this drawing of 1780 shows the Tollcross area before Lothian Road was built. The street leading towards the Castle in the centre of the drawing is now called High Riggs and the open area at its head is what we now term Tollcross. It was within a matter of only forty years that the open countryside in the foreground had become completely built up.

use of the name in its current position may have been influenced by the developing crossroads during the eighteenth and nineteenth centuries this is certainly not the whole story. Tollcross is a fairly large area of land and, if we are right in assuming that the Toll was originally at the Main Point, then we have to look closer at influences upon the crossroads area which may have helped to compound the use of the name at this point.

Going back to the Weir family, which for at least four generations possessed the south croft of Tollcross, it can be seen from the earliest Street Directories (from 1773) that it was one of the few described as living in 'Tollcross' (see Appendix I for 1786–8 directory where there are no references). Even so, the description 'Tollcross' is not used consistently, as can be seen for the entries for James Weir, the architect, and Jean Stuart Weir, his daughter-in-law:

1775/76 James Weir, wright, Lochrin
1777/78 James Weir, wright, Tollcross
1778/79 James Weir, wright, Tollcross
1784/85 Mrs Weir, Cowfeeder Row
1788/90 Mrs Weir, Tollcross
1790/92 Mrs Weir, Tollcross
1793/94 Mrs Weir, Tollcross
1795/96 Mrs Weir, Lochrin

Clearly the position of their house, situated between Riego Street and Earl Grey Street, could be described in a number of ways, which suggests that it was merely a reference point to locate a family living in a sparsely populated area. It also suggests that the name Tollcross did not apply to the position of the house but refers to the lands of Tollcross upon which it was built.

Looking at maps of a similar period an equally confused but interesting pattern emerges. The street we now call High Riggs is called variously:

Two-penny Custom (Arnot 1779)
Cowfeeder Row (Williamson 1784/85)
Two-penny Custom (Brown and Watson 1793)
Tollcross (Aitchison 1794/95)
Tollcross (Aitchison 1800/01
Tollcross (Stranger's Guide 1816)
Tollcross (Arnott 1825)
High Riggs (Post Office 1826)
Cowfeeder Row (Lothian 1829)
Tollcross; Hamilton Palace; High Riggs; Cowfeeder Row;
Two-penny Custom, in different sections (Lancefield 1851)

This was not the first street to be called after the lands of Tollcross. In Major James Weir's time, before his death in 1820, Riego Street had been laid, but was unnamed on Kirkwood's map of 1817. Although map references to a previous name are not available it seems it was originally called Tollcross Street. By 1823 we come across a sasine to William Henderson, millwright, and Andrew Pettrie, wright, 'on the north side of Tollcross Street'. A sasine of 1825 deals with Peter Stirling, horse dealer, concerning 'Tollcross Street or Riego Street'. The name Tollcross Street disappears completely by 1832

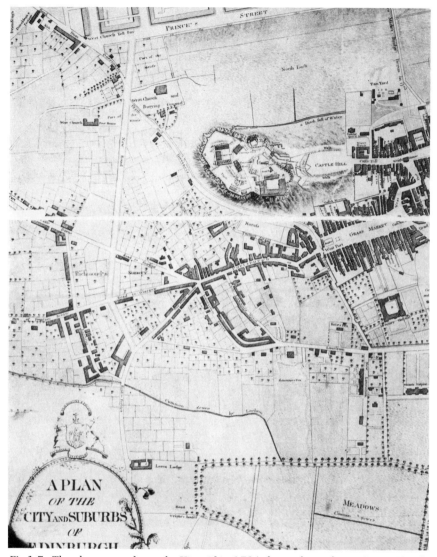

Fig 1.7: The above map drawn by Kincaid in 1784 shows the architect, James Weir's feu at the corner of Lothian Road (completed in 1788). The west end of Lauriston Place, at that time no more than a lane, is unnamed. The name 'Tollcross' is not in evidence either.

with reference to James Haig and son of Lochrin, in connection to property at 'Tollcross Street, now called Riego Street'.

Returning to Kirkwood's map of 1817 the name 'Tollcross' is to be found in a different position, referring to housing on the north side of modern day

Home Street and the foot of the High Riggs, broken by Earl Grey Street, at that time still called Lothian Road. One would be forgiven for thinking that this referred to the crossroads but in 1817 there is no Brougham Place, no west Tollcross, and Lauriston Place joined the High Riggs too far to the east to appear as one of the 'spokes of the wheel' description we can attach to the crossroads of today. Besides, in the 1823–4 Street Directory we find the first numbered reference to a Dr and Mrs Henderson at No 4 Tollcross.

By 1841 it is clear that the name Tollcross on the 1817 map referred to a street by that name which described housing only on the north side of Home Street and High Riggs. On the south side of the street there were no buildings in 1817 and by 1820 that side of the street was named Home Street and included numbers 1–17 at the foot of Lauriston Place on the same side of the street.

The Census returns of 1841 makes the picture much clearer by describing what appeared to be a crossroads as:

> Tollcross from Lochrin to Earl Grey Street (10 households, not numbered)
> and,
> Tollcross from Earl Grey Street to Riego Street (10 households, numbers 1–5 inclusive).

The street called Tollcross, clearly numbered and split by Lothian Road, appears in subsequent Census returns as Tollcross (east), numbers 1–5 inclusive, and Tollcross (west), numbers (varying every ten years) 1–12 inclusive. (A better description would be to call them the streets called Tollcross.) By 1891 only Tollcross (west) remains and, in the Street Directory of 1887 we find that Tollcross (east) has been incorporated into Lauriston Place and by 1897 Tollcross (west) into Home Street.

Around the same time that Tollcross (west) disappears, a new road is developed to give better access to Tollcross Tram Depot and the new Methodist Central Hall, built between 1898 and 1901. This street is, at first, called (west) Tollcross and by 1906 it is referred to as the West Tollcross that we see today.

From this evidence it seems more likely that the modern crossroads took its name from the streets called Tollcross and they, in their turn, from the lands which stretched to the north. It is significant that all of these streets were situated on the southern borders of these lands, much in the same way that the modern High Riggs marks the border of the lands of the same name, and Orchardfield (now Bread Street) as the border of those lands, described earlier.

That the name has continued to describe the vicinity where the Weir house stood suggests that Major James Weir (at least) had some influence over the naming of streets in the area, especially when we remember that he also lived at Lyndoch Place.

However, other influences were at work during the nineteenth century. Although Lothian Road remained for a long time the only significant departure to the roadway system in the area until the 1780s, by 1859 Brougham Place had been built and a route through the Meadows developed. By the

1870s Tollcross had become an important road junction and, with the coming of large scale horsedrawn and later, mechanised transport, in the shape of trams, the name Tollcross would have been the best reference to use at the crossroads, not just because one of the streets was so called at this point, but because of its singular sound.

In conclusion then it would appear that the origin of the name Tollcross is not as straightforward as it first seems. While it does seem controversial to suggest that the Toll, if there ever was one, was situated at the Main Point, and not at Tollcross as we know it, there is no evidence at all to the contrary. However, regardless of the position of the Toll, the development of the name at the crossroads does appear to have been influenced more by the previous street names than by the name of the lands of Tollcross.

What is certain, however, is that the history of Tollcross, from mediaeval times to modern day, has been an ever-changing scene, from orchard lands to a residential area, from a developing communications link to a busy industrial centre. Regardless of the exact meaning and position of Tollcross, its history remains one of the most fascinating in Edinburgh, and one with which for anyone living or working in the area can be proud to be associated.

Further reading

1 Boog Watson, C B. *Notes, Volumes 1–15*. Manuscript. Edinburgh Room, Central Public Library, Edinburgh.
2 Colvin, Howard, (1978). *Biographical Dictionary of British Architects 1600–1840*.
3 Dunlop, Alison Hay, (1890). *Anent Old Edinburgh*.
4 Forbes Gray, W, (1938). *Lothian House: a commemorative brochure*.
5 Geddie, John, (1911). *The Sculptured Stones of Edinburgh (IV Wrychtis Housis)*. Book of the Old Edinburgh Club (BOEC), **4**.
6 Gordon, James, (1782). *Catalogue of Shrubs and Flowers*. Edinburgh Room, Central Public Library, Edinburgh.
7 Heddle, R G, (1983). *Road Administration in Midlothian in the Early Eighteenth Century*. BOEC, **34**, pt 3.
8 Malcolm, C A, (1925). *The Gardens of the Castle*. BOEC, **14**.
9 Patterson, Andrew, (1966). *Tollcross to Morningside in the Olden Days*. BOEC, **32**.
10 Smith, John, (1932). *Notes on the Lands and Manor of Dalry*. Manuscript. Edinburgh Room, Central Public Library, Edinburgh.
11 Smith, John, (1932). *Notes of the Lands of High Riggs, Drumdryan and Tollcross*. BOEC, **18**.
12 Smith, John, (1935). *Dalry House: its lands and owners*. BOEC, **20**.

2

Growing Pains

Mary MacDonald

Portsburgh Roots

This chapter describes how a small ancient burgh at the western gate of the city, with its surrounding area of estates and country houses—described in the last chapter—became a part of the modern city. It was to a great extent an underprivileged part, in regard to housing and health; but it was also a part where important industries were developed, and where important institutions were set up to deal with the health problems of the whole city and even further afield. Industry is dealt with in the next chapter; this one concentrates on the social and health questions.

Quite a large part of the area, bounded on the south and west by Bruntsfield Links, Home Street and Leven Street, was within the burgh of barony known as Wester Portsburgh. But the populous part of that Burgh was, until the late eighteenth century, confined to the West Port with its side closes and wynds running east-west from the Vennel to the Main Point, which was the junction of the approach roads to the city from Stirling, Glasgow and Moffat. The rest of the Tollcross area was thinly populated.

The house still existing at the Main Point, No 4 High Riggs, occupied on the ground floor by the Burke and Hare Bar, was built in 1770 with an elegant facade. It was described as a 'gusset house', which aptly indicated its important position at the point of a triangle with main roads on either side.

Wester Portsburgh formed one burgh with Easter Portsburgh, which lay beyond Potterrow, but the two had separate, parallel administrations, each with its own bailies and incorporated trades. The origins of the burgh dated back to 1160 when John Abbot of Kelso granted to Laurence, son of Edmund of Edinburgh, a toft situated between the West Port and the castle on the left of the entrance to the city. At that time—and until much later—burghs were to a large extent trading organisations, with special privileges conferred by charter on the trades and crafts operated within them. A burgh of barony had a feudal superior, and was thus in a less independent position than a royal burgh such as Edinburgh. Indeed Portsburgh became in effect a dependency of Edinburgh when in 1648 the magistrates of Edinburgh purchased the superiority from Sir Adam Hepburn whose family had purchased it from the Touris family of Inverleith.

A full and picturesque account of Wester Portsburgh, founded in part on a study of the burgh records, is given by A H Dunlop, *Anent Old Edinburgh*. The situation of the burgh gave it importance as an access to the city. Dunlop quotes a detailed eye-witness account of a pageant with which Charles I was greeted on his entry to the city by the West Port. The burgh was also an important trading centre. It was pre-eminent in leather work, due to the proximity of the cattle market at the west end of Grassmarket and in Kings Stables Road (positioned there by James III in 1477, according to a plaque in the Grassmarket). The corn market, also nearby in the Grassmarket, gave facilities for baking. Dunlop describes in detail the armorial bearings of the burgh's six incorporated trades, which were: hammermen; tailors; cordiners (shoemakers); baxters (bakers); weavers; wrights and masons.

Fig 2.1: Detail from Gordon of Rothiemay's map of 1646 called 'A Bird's Eye View of Edinburgh', showing the suburbs of Wester Portsburgh, the Barras to the north and St Cuthbert's Church to the north west.

The burgh had magistrates, appointed by the Edinburgh magistrates—although Dunlop says that latterly some of them were elected by popular vote. They had some administrative powers and minor criminal jurisdiction. There was a court house with impressive furnishings—demolished in 1881 in the course of improvements—and even a prison.

During the late eighteenth century the whole area to the south of Edinburgh began to be built up. There was need for lighting, cleansing, watching—a whole range of local government functions which in those days went under the name of 'police'. Such functions were, in burghs, to some extent performed by the magistrates—but somewhat ineffectively. So a typical solution was to provide for the election by local residents of 'police commissioners', financed from a local rate.

So in 1771 an Act was passed stating that 'several streets . . . adjoining the City of Edinburgh on the south side thereof . . . are at present ill cleaned and not duly lighted and watched'. The Act divided these streets into eight districts. Commissioners for each district were to be elected, with the functions of watching, cleansing, lighting, removal of obstructions and prevention of nuisances, and with power to impose penalties and to levy a rate. they could also 'dispose of the street dung or fulzie' and apply the money thus raised to the purposes of the Act. Interim commissioners were appointed by name, except for three districts—including Tollcross—which were too thinly inhabited to raise funds for putting the Act into execution.

This system of police commissioners was extended, by an Act of 1805, to the whole city of Edinburgh and surrounding districts. Tollcross, including West Port, became the sixth ward. Further revisions were made in 1812 and 1822. Then in 1832 came the historic Act of Parliamentary reform in which the boundaries of Edinburgh were defined for Parliamentary purposes. They included Tollcross. An Act of the same year laid down the boundaries for police purposes to correspond with the Parliamentary boundaries. Finally, in 1856, the municipal boundaries for all purposes were extended to correspond with those of the Parliamentary burgh, and the powers of the police commissioners were transferred to the Magistrates and Council of the City of Edinburgh.

Housing and Hovels

Meanwhile great social changes were occurring. With the building of the New Town, the Bridges and Castle Terrace, the importance of the West Port as an access to the city had dwindled. At the same time the better off people had moved into the New Town, and large numbers of Irish workers, employed on building the Union Canal and other public works, were moving in. The result was serious overcrowding in the West Port, as well as in other parts of the Old Town such as the Grassmarket and High Street.

Lurid accounts were written of conditions in the wynds. Some of these (eg Stark Inquiry into the Sanitary State of Edinburgh 1847) show a tendency to attribute all the evils to the Irish immigrants. Many forms of anti-social behaviour, from pig-keeping through intemperance to non-payment of rent, are attributed to them. This reaction to migrant workers is an all too familiar one; and (as pointed out by Handley *The Irish In Scotland*) many of the evils described could have been the effect, rather than the cause of the bad conditions.

Lodging houses were early identified as a problem. Migrant workers and others who did not have a regular wage, and so could not pay a rent, crowded into these places—many of them in the West Port—where the charge was by the night. It was from a lodging house in Tanner's Close off the West Port—run by Hare—that Burke and Hare planned their murders in the 1820s, smothering victims who, they thought, were not likely to be missed and selling their bodies to the School of Anatomy. These 'dreadful Irish murders' were yet another stain on the reputation of the migrants, although Burke, according to Lord Cockburn, was by no means the intemperate pig-keeping Irishman. 'Except that he murdered' (rather a large exception) 'Burke was a sensible, and what might be called a respectable man; not at all ferocious in his general manner, sober, correct in all his other habits, and kind to his relations.'

Efforts were made to deal with the problem. An Act of 1822 contained provisions to regulate lodging houses, fixing maximum numbers for the inhabitants and providing for inspection. In 1841 the Edinburgh Lodging House Association was formed and its first building, a renovated lodging house in West Port, was opened in 1844 to accommodate seventy men. Later the same Association opened houses in Cowgate and Merchant Street. But these measures can have made only a small impact on the problem, for Bell, *Day and Night in the Wynds of Edinburgh*, 1849, describes among other horrors a place at the bottom of West Port where 'the worst characters lodge . . . from 4 to 8 or 10 persons can be accommodated in each apartment, which is locked, and the key kept by the landlord'. He also visited a room 12 feet by 10 feet where twelve women were asleep on the boards.

Dr Henry Littlejohn, recently appointed to the new post of Medical Officer of Health, in his classic *Report on the Sanitary Conditions of Edinburgh 1865* gives a much more optimistic picture. By an Act of 1848 lodging houses had been put under police surveillance. Regular visits, he says, were being made to see that the permitted number of lodgers was not exceeded; and he even suggests that epidemic disease had been kept under control by the enforcement of the regulations. However, it is hard to believe that bad conditions did not still exist.

By 1888, when the Corporation's Public Health Department issued a report on common lodging houses, the problem had abated somewhat, due to falling demand. but even then, out of sixty-two houses in the city only eighteen were described as 'in good order and clean'. Many were in bad structural condition. In the West Port there were seven houses, accommodating 414 lodgers.

Another problem highlighted by Littlejohn was that of purpose-built slums. Most of the overcrowded tenements were old houses, but he described two— Birtley Buildings, Canongate, and Crombie's Land at 50 West Port—that were modern. They were 'good examples of what would become of our courts and

Fig 2.2: Interior of Crombie's Land at 50 West Port. A drawing by Jane Stuart Smith, 1868.

closes, should proprietors be allowed to run up skeleton houses of the most rickety description and faulty sanitary construction. . . Both are inhabited by the very poor . . . each room is small and overcrowded; the passages are dark and ill-ventilated . . . they are both modern structures, built specially for the poor and with an eye to a large rental'. . . In Crombie's Land there were twenty-seven rooms inhabited by seventy people—sixteen of them under five years old—with no sinks and no WCs.

Crombie's Land did not last long after this—but it secured some return for its owner. In 1868 it was purchased by the Town Council for £475, with a view to demolishing it as part of Lord Provost Chambers' improvement scheme.

This scheme originated in Littlejohn's report. In his view the narrow, airless wynds and closes were a danger to health and he recommended cutting wide new streets through some of them. Lord Provost Chambers carried through the scheme, which is commemorated in the naming of Chambers Street. Two parts of it affected Tollcross:

1 In the West Port, several old houses and tenements were taken down so as to widen the street and clear out spaces behind the houses; new tenements were built.

2 Lady Lawson's Wynd was widened, and was continued north of the West Port to join up with Spittal Street, forming the present Lady Lawson Street. This involved taking in part of the cattle market on the site of the Art College. New houses were built along the line of the street. The tenements still existing which were built under this scheme are numbers 137–157 West Port and 6–30 and 46–52 Lady Lawson Street.

In total, 2721 dwellings were removed by the City Improvement Trustees, but only 340 were built under their auspices. So what became of the displaced tenants? For the Clerk to the Trustees, giving evidence to the Royal Commission on Housing of the Working Classes 1884–85, the answer was simple:

Q—Then you have turned out a great number of the poor?
A—Yes, a great many.
Q—Where do you think they have gone?
A—There has just been a general shift upwards throughout the whole of the population . . . the very poor have gone to houses which again have been vacated for the new houses which have been erected in very great numbers.

This reply reflects the thinking which prevailed at that time: overcrowded areas might be cleared by the authorities, but the provision of new housing should be left to free enterprise, whether in the form of trading concerns, cooperative effort, charity, or combinations of these. The difficulty was that these arrangements never really catered for 'the very poor'. This was pointed out by the Commissioners in their report, which in due course led to legislation giving wider powers to local authorities to clear sites and to build and own houses.

Nevertheless one notable benefit was attributed to the Improvement Scheme: the death rate had fallen. To assess whether this attribution was wholly correct would require deeper study, but certainly the fall was striking.

Between 1863 and 1883, the death rate for Edinburgh fell from 25.67 to 18.72 per 1000. Rates for St Giles and other central wards took part in the fall, but were still high; more will be said of this later.

Meanwhile in Fountainbridge and surrounding areas a great deal of building was going on. As a result, from 1861 to 1881 the population of the area increased from 9880 to 14 417.

An early development in the field of artisan housing was Chalmers Buildings, a three-storey block in Fountainbridge accommodating thirty families, built in 1855 by Patrick Wilson for a Mr Matheson. A more ambitious development was undertaken by James Gowans, who in 1853 built Rosebank Cottages to designs by Alexander Macgregor. This scheme comprised thirty-six houses in two-storey terraces, those on the ground floor being approached through gardens, and the upper ones by an external stair with an elegant classical-style railing. Each flat contained a living room, two bedrooms, scullery and WC.

According to Henry Roberts, a housing expert of the time, 'the cost of these houses, said to average £222 each, places them at a rental of £12 to 16 guineas per annum which is above the means of any but highly paid working people'. This was admitted by Gowans himself, when as Lord Dean of Guild he gave evidence to the Royal Commission. 'The class I would prefer as tenants,' he said 'are excisemen, postmen, and men in permanent situations.' In 1855–56, according to the directory, his tenants included a mason, a joiner, a clerk, and the superintendent of Lothian Road station.

Next door to Rosebank Cottages is Rosemount Buildings, constructed by 'an association' (name not known) in 1859. This square block, built round a central court, comprised flats for ninety-six families, most having three rooms and a WC. At the corners were washhouses for the use of the tenants on each floor. The rents varied from £6.10s to £10.10s per annum. The brick facing of the building, unusual for Edinburgh, suggests the influence of similar schemes in England. These flats were modernised in 1980 and are now owned by the Fountainbridge Housing Association.

By 1863 a number of building associations were at work in the area: the Edinburgh Cooperative Building Society, the Fountainbridge Church Building Association, the Cricket Park Building Association and the Grove Park Building Company. The cost of three-apartment houses averaged about £135, and larger houses from £160 to £195—more modest than Rosebank Cottages but still beyond the means of unskilled workers, whose average pay in 1884 was 15s a week and whose position was not secure enough for them to consider house purchase.

By such schemes the skilled workers were well provided for: but what of lower cost housing? Gowans, showing his plans of Rosebank Cottages to the Royal Commission, added: 'I have plans on the same model, but smaller, to be provided for the unskilled labourer.' But he also said, somewhat inconsistently, 'I do not think we need to build more houses. If the old, solid buildings were put in order it would provide for the very poor.' This view was also taken by a charitable body, the Social Union, which rehabilitated old tenements for letting; and we read also, in a report of 1893 by a Lord Provost's committee, of 'a small scheme by Dr Gunning in the West Port' which consisted mainly of remodelled houses. Rents were from £3.4s to £7 per annum. But in 1885 a charity was set up with the aim of meeting the need by new building. This was the Edinburgh Association for Improving the Dwellings of the Poor. In 1887 work was commenced on a tenement on the south side of West Port (nos 62 to 76) of forty dwellings with a plunge bath on every flat, a couple of wash houses and a resident caretaker. It was built on the site of the former Cordiners' Trade Hall, and a stone over the main door bears their emblem inscribed:

> Behold how good a thing it is
> And how becoming well
> Together such as brethren are
> In unity to dwell.

This building is now part of a derelict block which is scheduled for redevelopment. It is to be hoped that the inscribed stone, a piece of West Port history, will continue to be displayed.

According to the 1893 report, the rents for these houses were:

> 1 room and small scullery—£6.10s per annum.
> 2 rooms and small scullery—£9.2s per annum.

So the rents were still on the steep side for 'the very poor'.

And now the local authority began to make some use of their extended powers under the Housing of the Working Classes Act 1890. The overcrowded areas in the Tollcross district included Thornybauk and Ponton Street as well as West Port. In 1893, 202 houses were demolished in Thornybauk under an improvement scheme. There was said to be high mortality in the area, which the local people themselves attributed to the proximity of the slaughterhouse. In 1902, among a number of housing schemes in the city was Portsburgh Square in West Port with sixty-one houses—forty-nine of one apartment, and twelve of two apartments. The total building cost was £5829.5s.3d,

Fig 2.3: Present day photograph of 70 West Port, built in 1890, with a carved stone above the door depicting the Cordiners' emblem of 1606.

an average of just under £96 per house. These were clearly intended to meet the needs of poorer folk than Rosebank cottages, but the Burgh Engineer was being just a bit too cost-conscious when he decided on unplastered brickwork for the internal walls. This economy attracted much criticism. Portsburgh Square was modernised in 1978–80 and is now, with the rest of the north side of West Port, occupied as housing.

So ends the tale of Victorian housing, which transformed Tollcross from a sparsely populated suburb to a crowded part of the inner city. Today the overcrowding has largely been overcome, but, sadly, the thriving community built up by the nineteenth century development of artisan housing has also diminished as the character of the area has changed. Happily Rosebank Cottages, Rosemount Buildings and parts of Grove Street (as well as older properties such as Gardner's Crescent) are still occupied as dwellings, but in the street of Fountainbridge itself, industry and other uses have almost completely taken over. In 1926 there were ninety-one houses in the street, occupied by 793 parliamentary electors (*ie* adult population), in 1985 there were nine houses with eighty-five electors.

Life and Death

This brings us to another topic: mortality and disease, and their relation to living conditions. The conditions, as we have shown, varied greatly from one part of the Tollcross area to another. This is brought out by the details of the fall in death rates which, as mentioned earlier, took place between 1863 and 1883:

Edinburgh	25.67 to 18.72
Fountainbridge	25.20 to 18.72
St Giles	28.80 to 22.24

Throughout the nineteenth century the death rates for St Giles, which comprised the most overcrowded central areas including the West Port, remained consistently the highest in the city. This trend continued until the 1930s when it became less consistent.

Infant mortality tells the same tale. In 1909 the rate for the city was 113 per 1000, St Giles was the highest ward with 173; the lowest was 63. But in some parts of St Giles the rate was even higher. In 1908 the Medical Officer of Health had made a more detailed survey of certain areas which showed a rate of 214 for Grassmarket, West Port and adjacent streets.

Tuberculosis—especially pulmonary tuberculosis, also known as consumption or phthisis—was the main killer of adults, often of young adults. Details of this are given below, in the section on the Royal Victoria Dispensary. In 1899 the Medical Officer of Health reported a death rate from pulmonary consumption in St Giles ward of 2.45, compared with 1.92 for Edinburgh as a whole.

Many diseases were endemic—for example typhus, a disease which is borne by lice and is an index of poverty and poor living conditions. There were some cases nearly every year until 1907. *The 2nd Statistical Account, 1845*, says: 'Typhus appeared as an epidemic in 1814–15. Since then it has prevailed with more or less virulence every winter and is never entirely extirpated from the poorer dwellings'. Epidemics also occurred such as cholera, smallpox, and a disease vaguely described as 'fever'. Littlejohn, 1865, says: 'The history of all our epidemics of fever has been that, on the first outbreak of the disease, the Irish suffer in the first instance . . . congregated as they are in lodging houses.'

Such were the problems of the nineteenth century which did not, of course, all go away as the twentieth century dawned. Tuberculosis in particular remained a scourge until the 1950s. Our health problems today are different but we do have better equipment and knowledge to deal with them, for which thanks are due in large measure to the nineteenth-century pioneers of health care.

Health problems arose from trades practised in the area, as well as from living conditions. Most of these were common throughout the city—such as byres under dwellings, some of them dirty and housing diseased cows. Strangely enough, Littlejohn did not put much stress on this as a health problem. He must surely have been wrong—understandably, since in 1865 the tubercle bacillus had not yet been discovered. In the West Port and some other parts of Tollcross, owing to the proximity of the cattle market in Lauriston Place, particular problems arose with slaughterhouses and associated trades.

There had been slaughterhouses in the area at least since 1654, when the burgh records show that they were being provided 'within the West Port and at the north side thereof'. This was, at that time, on the edge of the populous area. Along with the slaughterhouses went trades, such as leatherwork for which West Port was renowned. Tanneries, even if not a health problem, were very offensive.

In the 1840s the Inspector of Lighting and Cleansing gave a gruesome account of the slaughterhouse called the 'Shambles' at King's Stables—the largest in Edinburgh. Offensive smells arose from the collection of blood and manure, and the drainage was defective. There were four tanyards in the neighbourhood. Two doctors gave evidence on the prevalence of epidemic disease in the area. There were other slaughterhouses in West Port, besides a group in Cowfeeder Row (High Riggs) and one in Drumdryan.

All this changed with an Act of 1850 which provided that slaughtering was to take place only in the public slaughterhouse. This was erected in 1851 in Fountainbridge, on the site of the Lochrin distillery, to the design of David Cousin, City Architect. Cousin's work has adorned Edinburgh in a number of styles, including Jacobean (Free Church Offices) Italianate (Reid School of Music) Scots Renaissance (India Buildings) and others, but so far as we know, the splendid facade of the slaughterhouse was his only essay in the Ancient Egyptian manner. It was demolished about 1912, and Tollcross Primary School was erected on the site.

As the century went by, the public slaughterhouse itself became a problem. This is described in a fifty years review of Edinburgh's public health, published

Fig 2.4: Top hats at the Egyptian gate in front of the municipal slaughterhouse in Fountainbridge before 1912.

by the Town Council in 1950. It states that Littlejohn 'recommended the removal of the slaughterhouse and the cattle market at Lauriston Place to sites apart from dwellings'. He considered that mortality in the adjoining streets had been affected.

Littlejohn's advice was heeded, and a slaughterhouse was built at Gorgie. The dead meat markets at Fountainbridge and Ponton Street continued in use until 1955, by which time they were 'old, badly lit, and during the summer months poorly ventilated'. In the hot summer of 1955 large quantities of meat had to be condemned. Accordingly, the Corporation took power to build a meat market at Gorgie.

Health Care

The story of our area's health problems over past years makes sad reading. But when we move on to health care we get a much more enlivening story: one of active pioneering effort which brought benefits far beyond the boundaries of Tollcross, in some cases worldwide. In part the location of these developments in Tollcross was fortuitous, because sites for institutions happened to be available there; but in part, as with Dr Philips' tuberculosis dispensary, the developments were sited in the overcrowded central city area because they were most needed there. Whatever the causes may have been, the result is to make Tollcross an area of great interest from this aspect.

The Royal Infirmary of Edinburgh
First and foremost—in age, renown and sheer bulk—comes the Royal Infirmary. Although its present location in the Tollcross area dates only from 1879, its origin goes back to 1729 when it was opened in a small house with six beds in what is now Infirmary Street. In 1736 a charter was obtained, and in 1748 a new building, also in Infirmary Street, was completed. In 1832 a surgical hospital was opened in High School Yards nearby, and in 1854 the 'New Surgical Hospital' was added. Clinical teaching took place from the outset, thus establishing a link with Edinburgh University and the Royal Colleges of Physicians and Surgeons.

Eventually the buildings became inadequate. Cross infection was also a problem because of poor ventilation, so after much controversy it was decided to rebuild on a more open site in Lauriston Place. The buildings and grounds of George Watson's Hospital were acquired, and in 1879 the new building was opened. It was designed by David Bryce in the Scots Baronial style; Florence Nightingale's principles of open layout were adopted and her approval obtained. George Watson's buildings were retained to provide administrative accommodation. The old medical hospital was demolished in 1884, but the surgical hospitals still stand—in Drummond Street, named after George Drummond who was prominent in founding the Infirmary. They are now owned and occupied by Edinburgh University.

From there on the Infirmary grew and developed. Other institutions too were developing and taking part of the load. The City Fever Hospital moved to its present site in Colinton Mains in 1903. It took on the care of infectious diseases, and later other facilities as well. In 1930 the old poor law institutions became local authority hospitals; three of them became the Western, Northern and Eastern General Hospitals, which two years later were designated as teaching hospitals. Thus began the development of the Western General to become coequal with, and complementary to, the Royal Infirmary. But there was plenty of scope for all. New services and specialties proliferated, many of them calling for extensions to the fabric.

In 1948 the Infirmary became part of the National Health Service, financed from public funds. Previously it had been supported by voluntary subscriptions, donations and legacies from the public, to such good effect that in 1948 its endowment fund stood at £1 283 900—nearly ten per cent of the total for Scottish hospitals, with only two per cent of the beds. There was a League of Subscribers, and groups of workers, such as miners, made regular contributions. Part of this endowment fund was distributed after 1948 to other hospitals, but the Infirmary retained a substantial part for financing improvements.

Voluntary service to the Infirmary did not cease in 1948. Today the Edinburgh Royal Infirmary Samaritan Service works in cooperation with the Social Work Department in helping patients. The Royal Infirmary Volunteers provide help within the hospital, such as canteen and trolley services.

By the NHS scheme of 1948 the Infirmary was grouped under a Board of Management with several other hospitals. In 1974 there was a reorganisation of the NHS under which Boards of Management were abolished and all hospitals are now administered by the Health Board.

So what of the future? The buildings of 1879 are old-fashioned and cluttered with additions. The 1981 block next door is entitled 'Phase 1'. So Phases 2, 3 and onwards will be—where? and when? This is the subject of current debate.

The Royal Edinburgh Hospital for Sick Children
This Hospital, now situated in Sciennes Road to the south of the Meadows, had its beginnings in the Lauriston area.

The need for a children's hospital in Edinburgh was brought to public attention during the 1850s by two doctors, Charles Wilson and John Smith. An article in *The Scotsman* put the case succinctly: 'The mixing-up of sick children with sick adults is a deteriorating arrangement, yet worse in many ways is the retention of these little ones in their miserable homes.'

In 1859 an appeal for subscriptions was launched, and met with success. After considering various locations a house was selected at 7 Lauriston Lane— a street now swallowed up by Royal Infirmary extensions, which ran from Lauriston Place to the Meadows, east of Archibald Place. Objections—of a kind still familiar—from neighbours, who did not want a hospital so near them, were surmounted. The house was leased, was adapted to accommodate twenty-four in-patients together with an out-patient department, and was opened as a hospital in February 1860. It had a distinguished medical staff, including Dr Graham Weir, who had made a special study of the hospital system on the continent, and who served the hospital for twenty-eight years until his retiral at the age of seventy-six. He died in 1896.

The number of patients—especially fever patients—soon made the accommodation inadequate. To replace it, Meadowside House, a property at the foot

Fig 2.5: Portrait of Dr T Graham Weir whose family lived in Tollcross for a number of generations and who was one of the original medical staff at The Royal Hospital for Sick Children.

of Lauriston Lane facing on the the Meadows, was purchased. It was adapted as a hospital with forty-four beds—including twelve fever beds—and an out-patient department. In May 1863 it was opened, under Queen Victoria's patronage, as the Royal Edinburgh Hospital for Sick Children.

In 1870 an extension was built to provide an additional thirty-six beds. In 1885, when the City Fever Hospital was established in the old Infirmary building, the Sick Children's Hospital ceased to admit fever cases. But in spite of these reliefs there was still a need for more beds. Things came to a head in 1890 when an outbreak of typhoid among the staff gave rise to doubts about the sanitary condition of the hospital. The patients and staff were removed to Morningside College at Plewlands. An inspection of Meadowside House showed that the facilities there were inadequate, and it was demolished.

The original intention was to rebuild on the same site, but this was required for extensions to the Royal Infirmary. Accordingly, the Sick Children's Hospital, accommodating initially 120 in-patients, was established in 1895 on its present site in Sciennes Road—formerly the site of the Trades Maiden Hospital, a school for girls founded by Mary Erskine. At the opening ceremony it was stated that 180 000 sick children had benefited from the institution since its foundation.

The Royal Victoria Dispensary
One of the worst health problems of town life in the nineteenth century—indeed well into the twentieth—was tuberculosis, especially of the lung (consumption). Figures for 1899, given by Dr Littlejohn, show the extent of the problem. In that year there were 790 deaths in Edinburgh from tuberculosis, of which 574 were pulmonary (consumption). The total death rate from tuberculosis was 2.64 per 1000 population, or 14.64 per cent of the total mortality from all causes. The average age of the consumption victims was thirty-three; more than three-fifths of them lived in houses of one, two or three rooms. Cases were thickly clustered in the central areas, including West Port and Fountainbridge.

In 1882 the bacteriologist Robert Koch identified the tubercle bacillus as the cause of tuberculosis. The significance of this was quickly appreciated by an Edinburgh physician, Dr Robert W Philip: if the disease was caused by an organism it could be prevented. The task of preventing or, at least, controlling its spread was enormous and was not fully achieved until the mid twentieth century with the aid of new drugs and techniques and improved standards of living. But Dr Philip was the pioneer.

Treatment for tuberculosis had up to then been confined to the relief of acute symptoms. In 1887 Dr Philip opened a dispensary, in three rooms up a stair in Bank Street, where efforts were also made to control the spread of the disease. He obtained the support of a committee, and trustees were appointed who appealed for funds, thus enabling the dispensary to move, in 1891, to better premises at 26 Lauriston Place.

Dr (later Sir Robert) Philip had a definite plan of campaign against tuberculosis. It included the provision of a centre for information and advice; careful investigation and recording of each case; instruction of each patient in self-treatment and control of infection; home visiting by doctor and nurse; selection of cases for in-patient care. This became known as 'the Edinburgh system' and was later a model for other areas. But it called for more hospital beds. Once again the trustees appealed for funds and in August 1894 the Victoria Hospital was opened in Craigleith Road. In 1904 it was granted Royal patronage under the name of 'The Royal Victoria Hospital for Consumption'. A farm colony was also established at Polton where patients who were fit enough could work in the open air.

The Town Council, as local health authority, set aside beds in the City Hospital for advanced cases. Then in 1911 came the National Insurance Act which made local authorities responsible for dealing with tuberculosis. The Royal Victoria Dispensary and Hospital were handed over by the Trustees to the Town Council. A tuberculosis officer was appointed, with Dr Philip as consultant, and the Town Council adopted the Edinburgh system. A former church in Spittal Street was converted into new premises for the dispensary;

these premises still house the Area Chest X-Ray Unit maintained by the Lothian Health Board.

Dr Philip died in 1939, too early to see the resurgence of tuberculosis after the Second World War and the measures, eventually successful, which were taken to deal with it.

Chalmers Hospital

George Chalmers, plumber, on his death in 1836 left £27 000 to the Faculty of Advocates to found an infirmary. This sum was allowed to accumulate until 1854 when Lauriston House and ground was purchased. The hospital, designed by J Dick Peddie, was commissioned in 1864. It continued to be managed by the Faculty of Advocates—who appointed a Board of Directors for the purpose—until it became part of the NHS in 1948.

In 1872 two wards were opened for paying patients. Their fees, together with donations and contributions from capital, financed the hospital; no public appeals were made for funds. No paying patients were admitted after 1948.

In 1924 the hospital was recognised as a training school and in 1933 a new wing was added.

In 1951 the Hospital for Diseases of Women, in Archibald Place, with forty beds, was incorporated as an annexe. This had been opened as a nursing home in 1900, was managed by a voluntary organisation from 1910 and handed over to the NHS in 1951. It was demolished in 1968 to make way for an Infirmary extension.

In 1961 a general practice unit was added to the hospital.

The Royal Simpson Memorial Maternity Hospital (now Pavilion)

A few maternity beds were provided in the Royal Infirmary from 1755 to 1793. In that year the Edinburgh General Lying-in Hospital was founded. Fifty years later it became the Edinburgh Royal Maternity Hospital, but not till 1879 did it acquire purpose-built accommodation on the south side of Lauriston Place, erected as a memorial to Sir James Y Simpson. Here notable pioneer work in anaesthetics was done. In 1901 Dr J W Ballantyne arranged for a bed to be endowed—the first bed in the world specifically set aside for antenatal care and studies. In the next decade Dr J Haig Ferguson started the first antenatal clinic in Great Britain. It was his experience as visiting physician to the pre-maternity home for unmarried mothers—opened in 1899, latterly located at 4 Lauriston Park and named the Haig Ferguson Memorial Home—which had brought home to him the value of antenatal care. 'From these beginnings,' says E S Catford 'acceptance of the need for systematic antenatal care grew and spread throughout the United Kingdom and across the world.'

In time the building became inadequate—indeed it was described as 'obstetrically a slum'—and the only practicable course was a merger with the Royal Infirmary, who launched an appeal for new building. The Simpson Memorial Maternity Pavilion in the Royal Infirmary complex, with 122 beds, was opened for patients in 1939—at the same time as the Florence Nightingale

Nurses' Home, which adjoins it. Since then the Simpson has played a leading part in the developments which have changed the whole aspect of maternity care, greatly reducing the rates of maternal and perinatal mortality.

Bruntsfield Hospital
The story of Bruntsfield Hospital is bound up with that of two pioneers, Sophia Jex-Blake and Elsie Inglis. Sophia, in 1869, applied for admission to the Medical Faculty of Edinburgh University, Six other women joined her and they obtained some limited admission to classes, but it was not till 1894 that women were allowed to graduate in medicine. Meanwhile Sophia had graduated MD at Berne and in 1878 she set up practice in Manor Place. In the same year she opened at 73 Grove Street 'The Provident Dispensary for Women and Children' where treatment could be obtained for a few pence. In 1885 it was moved to 6 Grove Street where five beds were provided. A committee of subscribers was formed and in 1899 they established the Edinburgh Hospital and Dispensary for Women and Children at Bruntsfield Lodge which had been Dr Jex-Blake's home. The inpatients from Grove Street were moved to the new hospital, but dispensary work continued, first at Torphichen Place and later again at Grove Street.

Meanwhile, also in 1899, a group of medical women on the initiative of Dr Elsie Inglis had opened a nursing home for women, 'The Hospice' in George Square. In 1903 it was transferred to 219 High Street. In 1910 the committees of the two hospitals amalgamated; the Hospice dealt with obstetrics and infants while the Bruntsfield had the medical, surgical and gynaecological departments. Each hospital retained its original name and continued to operate its own dispensary. Elsie Inglis died while tending the wounded in the First World War, and in 1925 the Elsie Inglis Memorial Hospital was founded in memory of her. The Hospice was closed, at an unknown date, possibly around this time.

Over these years the Bruntsfield Hospital had been much extended from its original twelve beds. In 1948 both hospitals became part of the National Health Service. Then controversy arose: in 1956 the Regional Hospital Board proposed to open the appointment of consultants at both hospitals to male applicants. The case was taken to the High Court, and an order obtained that a man should not be appointed unless and until the post had been advertised for women only and no suitable applicant obtained. The result, at that time, was the appointment of a women to the post of consultant physician to both hospitals; but since then there have been some male appointments.

The function of the Bruntsfield Hospital was changing. Some general medical and surgical facilities were withdrawn, but a gynaecological service was still provided. Then in 1984 the Lothian Health Board (successor to the Regional Hospital Board) proposed to close the hospital. Once again, as in 1956, the hospital's supporters rallied. Strong representations were made by the Bruntsfield Hospital Action Committee, and the proposal for closure was withdrawn. In 1988 its future is again in doubt.

Homes for Social Care

In the field of social care—for the old, the poor and the disadvantaged—three institutions for residential care have existed in Tollcross. One of them is long forgotten, one is within recent memory, and one is still meeting a pressing need today.

St Cuthbert's Charity Workhouse

This institution, which long predates the building up of the Tollcross area, stood on a site north of what is now the Sheraton Hotel. It was one of three which catered for Edinburgh and the surrounding districts, the others being in Forrest Road (the City Workhouse) and Canongate. Its catchment area was the extensive parish of St Cuthbert's.

The 2nd Statistical Account, 1845, describes the workhouse in some detail. It was opened in 1762 with 84 inmates and was enlarged at different times. It was managed first by the Kirk Session, then by a Board of Management drawn from heritors of the parish (later, following the Poor Law Act 1848, it came under the Parochial Board). In 1837 it had 539 inmates. They worked at shoemaking, joiner work, weaving, knitting, sewing and hairteasing, and there was a school with nearly 200 pauper children. A committee of ladies

Fig 2.6: Photograph of a carved stone taken from St Cuthbert's Charity Workhouse and now in the Huntly House Museum. The words on it are from the Apocrypha (Eccl IV:1):

My son defraud not the Poor of his living and make not the Needy Eyes
to wait long.

daily visited the female inmates to read the scriptures and converse on religious subjects. The heritors had purchased forty perpetual rights at £34 each for admission of lunatic paupers into the Royal Edinburgh Lunatic Asylum. However, there were—or at least had been a few years earlier, at the time of the 1841 census—some lunatics in the workhouse itself; for at that time the staff included John Nicolson (aged forty-one), Superintendent of Lunatic Asylum. The staff as a whole was rather a small one, consisting (in addition to Nicolson) of William Gray, Governor and Treasurer; Marie Lamb, Mistress; Alex Macdonald, Keeper of Funeretory; and Margaret Dishington, Assistant. All these were evidently supervisors, the day to day work being presumably done by the inmates, of whom there were at that time 301 adults—mostly from fifty to eighty years old—and 154 children.

By the 1860s the citizens were considering the removal of workhouses from the city centre. Littlejohn, in his 1865 report, favoured this idea. Although the site of St Cuthbert's was good, and was 'only now being surrounded by buildings', the structure was antiquated. Outdoor relief was only a pittance, but many of the persons claiming it 'will submit to the greatest privations rather than allow themselves to be immured within those barrack-like buildings . . . the confined dismal spaces allowed to the sexes as airing grounds only deepen the feeling'. If they had fresh country air and exercise 'residence in a workhouse would not be dreaded as it is at present'.

In this he was optimistic. For many years the stigma of a workhouse past still clung to premises, such as Craiglea Old People's Home and the Western, Northern and Eastern General Hospitals, which had been used for this purpose. Happily modern developments have now overlaid the memory of the past. The workhouse was finally demolished in 1870 to make way for expansion to the Caledonian Railway.

The Little Sisters of the Poor

A very different type of social care, religious in inspiration but in line with modern trends, is provided by the Little Sisters of the Poor in their Home for elderly people with low income, situated at 43 Gilmore Place. The Sisters have 275 Homes for the Aged throughout the world, of which four are in Scotland.

The Foundress of the Order, Jeanne Jugan (1792 to 1879) was a Breton woman, and the first Homes set up were in France. In the 1850s one was set up in London. The Edinburgh Home dates from 1865. In the 1881 census it had a staff of thirteen sisters, eight of whom (including the Mother Superior) came from France and one from Belgium. Of the inmates—61 male and 85 female—the majority were of Irish extraction.

Many of those who were helped by the Order in its early days had been obliged to beg for their bread until they became too old to do so. Jeanne Jugan put herself on an equal footing with these people by begging on their behalf. This practice of fundraising by the Sisters themselves asking for alms has been maintained by the Order. There is a 'Jeanne Jugan Organisation' which is interdenominational, and whose members collaborate with the Sisters in their work of caring for elderly people with low income.

The Edinburgh Home has been upgraded from time to time and now accommodates 66 residents in their own rooms. There is a visiting doctor and some of the sisters are qualified nurses. There is also a resident priest and a chapel for Catholic worship for those who wish, but the residents can be of all denominations. Recently the chapel has been altered so that the lower floor now accommodates a day centre.

Ponton House—the Edinburgh Home for Working Lads
Residential, institutionalised care for old people is still very much in demand, but for young people this type of care is now less favoured. A derelict, truncated but still impressive building at the corner of Ponton Street and Fountainbridge recalls how the need for such care was met in its time.

In 1867 Mr David J Harris founded a Home for fifteen lads taken off the street. For a very short period the lads were formed into a shoe black brigade which called itself the Edinburgh Industrial Brigade. The Home became known as the Edinburgh Industrial Brigade Home. In 1928 it became the Edinburgh Home for Working Lads.

The Home was for boys of school leaving age (14) and upwards who were capable of and willing to work. Many were homeless boys—referred from orphanages, industrial schools and so on—but the Home also accepted boys from the country whose parents could not afford to maintain them in Edinburgh while learning a trade. The boys paid over the bulk of their earnings, but this did not cover the cost. A good deal of charitable effort went into the Home, with a group of ladies doing sewing and mending, while 'lady collectors' raised funds.

Soon after its inception the Home adopted the principle of apprenticing each boy to a trade. Evening education was added, and recreation improved. Christian guidance was one of the Home's objects.

The Home started in Cockburn Street, and later was in an adapted tenement in Grove Street. Premises in Ponton Street, on the corner of Fountainbridge, were built in 1899–1900. In 1910 an extension—now demolished—was built. In 1952 the accommodation was modernised, giving bedrooms to the boys in place of dormitories.

In 1914 there were 126 boys in residence, but numbers were depleted by the First World War and in 1919 they were down to fifty-eight. They never again rose above a hundred. In the years of depression there was difficulty in finding skilled employment for the boys.

In 1962, with numbers down to about fifty, the Home moved to nos 6 and 7 Magdala Crescent, a street of large Victorian terraced houses. It remained there till 1977. By this time most of the residents were boys who had been referred by the Social Work Department as in need of residential care; and as the demand for this kind of care diminished, the Home ceased to be viable. It was therefore closed. Its remaining assets were used to found the Ponton House Association, which seeks to help and secure employment for disadvantaged young people of both sexes throughout Scotland who fall outwith the scope of Government schemes. The Association also provides other forms of assistance for specific approved cases.

Further reading

1 Bell, G, (1849). *Day and Night in the Wynds of Edinburgh.*
2 Boog Watson, C B, (1964). *A Short History of the Chalmers Hospital.*
3 Catford, E S, (1979). *The Royal Infirmary of Edinburgh, 1929–1979.*
4 Dunlop, A H, (1890). *Anent Old Edinburgh.*
5 Gifford, J, McWilliam, C, Walker, D, (1984). *The Buildings of Scotland—Edinburgh.*
6 Guthrie, Douglas, (1960). *The Royal Edinburgh Hospital for Sick Children 1860–1960.*
7 Littlejohn, H J, (1865). *Report on the Sanitary Conditions of Edinburgh.*
8 Logan Turner, L, (1929). *The Story of a Great Hospital—The Royal Infirmary of Edinburgh 1729–1929.*
9 Tarn, J H, (1971). *Working Class Housing in Nineteenth Century Britain.*

3

The Working Population

George Brown

Introduction

The history of industry in this part of the City can be traced back at least to the Incorporated Trades of Wester Portsburgh in the late middle ages and, in particular to the making of leather goods, for which the Burgh was famous.

The area around Tollcross has for many centuries been an important trading centre because of its position immediately outwith the ancient route to the Town of Edinburgh and the Castle. Road developments in the late eighteenth century (particularly Lothian Road in 1788, followed by a Canal terminus in 1822, and a Railway station in 1848) contributed radically to the growth of that industry. The main locus of industry rapidly drifted from the overcrowded West Port to the growing village of Fountainbridge which, by the end of the nineteenth century, was by far the most industrialised area of Edinburgh.

In 1910 a survey was carried out to determine how many people were employed in Fountainbridge. The following approximate figures were obtained and were published in the *Evening News*:

Rubber Works	4000
Vulcanite Works	300
Brewery	500
West End Engine Works	100
St Cuthbert's Cooperative	200
Walker and Sons	50
Marwick's Confectionery	40
Oil and Cake Mills	40
Meat Market, shop assistants, and other places of business	600
TOTAL EMPLOYED =	6000 approximately.

In this chapter an attempt has been made to cover the main industries of the area but it also includes many smaller concerns to illustrate the variety and complexity of industrial life from the eighteenth to the twentieth century. Unfortunately many industries have been left out through lack of space, the most important of which was the building industry, which included roads, the railway and the canal, as well as houses, shops and factories. Other businesses and services will be remembered by many of their former employees who worked at Martin's the Baker, Murchie's Creamery, The Tram and Bus depot, and Harris', who made hosiery at Lady Lawson Street for the big department stores—and many, many more. Others have been dealt with in other chapters, or in more detail than appears here.

Fig 3.1: The first shop belonging to St Cuthbert's Cooperative Society Association at 50 Fountainbridge, on the corner of Ponton Street, opened in 1859.

St Cuthbert's Cooperative Association

Introduction

Before we look at the history of the 'Store' we have to ask how did Cooperative Societies come about in the first place, especially in a society which had had a morbid fear of organised working people. Even as late as the 1820s all combinations of working men into Unions or Societies was considered seditious under a law, which was not repealed until 1825.

By the 1850s a shift of power had taken place in Society. The old landed Tories who had held control in Parliament were gradually displaced by men who had other interests than land. The repeal of the Corn Laws in this period indicated this change. Wealth from the new industries of the industrial revolution and from overseas trade flowed into the pockets of the new breed of politician, a more enlightened class, optimistic for the future of Britain and more liberal in their attitudes.

Early attempts at Cooperation had been doomed because their objectives were considered by temporary commentators as far too advanced and idealistic. Anyone who urged change in society throughout the nineteenth century was in danger of being considered Utopian by the establishment. These attempts, while defensible in their intent, were patently unrealisable, as they included widespread purchase of land, control of education and large scale cooperative supplies of food and other goods.

Success came with moderation. Cooperative Societies were deemed acceptable if they did not present a threat to authority—just as with the so called New Model Trade Unions of the same period. As long as they were duly constituted, with written objectives and rule books, they were entirely respectable features of Victorian Society. So, by limiting their objectives, the later Cooperatives proved themselves acceptable organisations.

The History of the 'Store'

In 1859, at a house in Grove Street, a group of twelve artisans met to discuss the possibility of founding a cooperative for buying and selling the necessities of life in the area around Fountainbridge. A number of these men worked alongside one another at the Edinburgh and Glasgow Railway Company's workshops at Haymarket and others at the adjacent cabinet works of Messrs J and T Scott. In the true spirit of optimism, with no funds available, the hopefuls registered their company as a Cooperative on 1 November 1859. To raise the registration fee of three guineas and other extras, the Committee had 500 copies of their rules printed, which were sold for 1d each.

Premises were acquired at 50 Fountainbridge, at the corner of Ponton Street, and St Cuthbert's Cooperative, or the 'Store', was in business on 4 November. A membership of sixty-three was immediately achieved and the initial paid up capital of the venture was just over £30.

The shop was sited intentionally as near to the Union Canal basin as possible, and close to its membership. One of the original Committee spoke later of his memories of the first days of the shop:

We were all yet working men, but we began to have the feeling that we were something more, and would soon be businessmen, reaping profits we had for long been sowing for others.

Great delight was shown when, after the first quarter, the members' books showed a profit of £13, and a dividend of 1s 1d in the pound was duly paid out. However, due to a clerical error, it was later realised that in fact the Association was £10.19s 3d in the red by the third quarter. Regardless of this set-back the pioneers showed great perseverance and by the seventh quarter the Society could boast a credit balance enough to pay back debts and a modest dividend to members of $2\frac{3}{4}$d in the pound on purchases.

The 'Store' now went from strength to strength. Due more to perseverance than professionalism and, despite the many set-backs, St Cuthbert's was to survive to become a respected business, trusted by merchants and customers alike. Gradually the founders, knowing little about the grocery trade, began to be replaced by professional shop managers, with the obvious benefit that this accrued.

Close association with, and being a founder member of the Scottish Cooperative Wholesale Society enabled the 'Store' to strengthen its position. Proof of the success of the Cooperative during its first fifty years can be seen from the membership of 1909 which had risen from sixty-three in the first year to over 40 000 by then. During this period the Association divided up its £3 646 726 profit among the members.

Fig 3.2: The catering staff at St Cuthbert's Cooperative in the 1930s.

A great part of this success was due to the business acumen of Alexander Mallace, General Manager between 1881 and 1911. During his term of employment he had presided over enormous expansion of the business. The Society had shops in every part of the City and beyond, selling everything from coal to butcher meat and drapery goods. The impressive headquarters in Fountainbridge and the Department Store in Bread Street were also built within this period. The Dividend had remained stable at the very acceptable sum of 4s 4d for many years and the 'Store' was regarded by many of Edinburgh's businessmen with great envy.

Within the next three years, from 1909 to 1912, St Cuthbert's Cooperative Association had achieved higher sales than any other in Britain and had expanded into farming, thereby growing a great deal of its shop produce. Corn grown was turned into flour at the SCWS Chancelot Mill at Bonnington.

The Dividend
Quarterly meetings of the Association were, to say the least, lively affairs. As all members were entitled to vote and to question the Board it became increasingly difficult to find premises large enough to contain the voters. It is hard to imagine how meetings were conducted and decisions reached when half the members met in one venue and half in another. This happened on a number of occasions. Worse still there was a tendency for differences of opinion to develop between the members meeting in one venue as opposed to the other, each side rallying its supporters to address the important issues of the day.

One such issue, which was to remain high on the agenda for a great number of years, was that of the Dividend versus Cheaper Prices debate. The Cheaper Prices camp argued that if one were a woman attempting to raise a family on £3 a week, the accrued dividend was less of a consideration than the initial cost of the goods. On the other hand if one were a Morningside matron who bought expensive articles from the Drapery Department the dividend would be a great consideration. Mr Mallace believed strongly that the original ideals of the Movement were to benefit the less well off and therefore supported the Cheaper Prices camp. In reality the issue was a great deal more complex as the well-off would benefit regardless of these considerations and, in later years, competition from other large business concerns forced the issue of the dividend into a corner. However, this state of affairs haunted the Movement until 1933. In that year the Board announced a Reduced Price Policy after many years of declining custom. The prices of butter, bacon, jam, cereals and eggs were lowered. As a result there was a forty-one per cent increase in sales within the first three months.

The Great Institution
St Cuthbert's continued to grow over the years. Through a policy of absorbing smaller Cooperative Societies it increased its membership and widened its outlets throughout eastern Scotland. In 1923 St Cuthbert's had the highest sales figures of any in Britain despite the fact that it was only the fifth highest in total membership. By 1925 after building the new bakery and dairy at

Port Hamilton, the membership stood at 71 000 with an annual turnover of £4 million.

Despite the hard year of 1926 when a four per cent decline in trade was recorded due to the General Strike, business soon recovered. By 1935 the 'Store' was the largest farm owner in Scotland, and by 1937 its membership had increased by nearly 10 000 over the previous ten years. A decade later St Cuthbert's is recorded as being the largest ratepayer in the city and also one of the largest employers, with a workforce of over three and a half thousand men and women. At the pinnacle of its success by the mid 1950s the Association registered its one hundred thousandth member and boasted acquired assets of three and a quarter million pounds.

In the first fifty years of this century many of the Association's major outlets were in the Tollcross and Fountainbridge area. At the headquarters site at 92 Fountainbridge were its offices, the grocery, bakery and butchery departments. At the East Fountainbridge and Bread Street Department Store were the central drapery, tailoring, dressmaking, millinery, furniture, upholstery, crockery, hardware, jewellery, grocery, drugs and paint departments—including a waitress service Tea Room. At 79–85 Morrison Street was a large grocer's, baker's and butcher's shop, and not far away there was a substantial coal depot at the goods station at the foot of Morrison Street. Other outlets included factories producing biscuits and sausages at High Riggs and Lauriston Street, as well as stables in Grove Street.

Through their forward-looking sales policies, successive Association Boards had built one of the greatest cooperative retailers in Britain with interests in the distribution of a wide variety of produce. Not only had it self-sufficiency in meat and milk production on a huge scale, it also offered many services to the community and to its own workforce. It supplied luxury coaches, funeral arrangements, premises for wedding receptions and retirement parties. In short it became an institution to its many members and non-members alike.

Over the last thirty years the Cooperative Movement has sadly declined in stature. Unfortunately competition from chain stores such as Marks and Spencer, British Home Stores and Littlewoods and multiple food retailers such as Asda, Safeway, Presto and Sainsbury, has been very damaging over the years and, although St Cuthbert's attempted to keep abreast of modern trends by building supermarkets, changing tastes and increasing prosperity proved strong factors in the success of its competitors.

In April 1988 demolition work started at the old bakery and dairy complex at Fountainbridge, opening up a huge site for the development of shops, offices and restaurants by a private developer. It is felt unlikely that this complex will recreate the energy and the community spirit for which the 'Store' was famous.

However, the 'Store', now called Scotmid, is still very much in business and we understand it would welcome a suitable opportunity to expand again in the Tollcross area. Meanwhile the capital realised on the sale of the redundant assets at Fountainbridge is being ploughed back into the development of modern superstores. Part of this redevelopment programme includes the work presently being carried out at the 92 Fountainbridge headquarters where internal renovation and external stone cleaning and restoration work is in progress. When this refurbishment work is completed, the 92 Fountainbridge complex will incorporate a completely new funeral parlour, travel bureau and computer department, indicative of the progressive attitude of the present Board of Directors and Management.

While the society's development within the Tollcross area is restricted by elements outwith its own influence, this is not to say that this temporary halt is a true reflection of its current trading position. In point of fact the society is currently enjoying an upturn in its fortunes unprecedented within the last decade. The previous three years have each seen the building of a major new superstore and a fourth superstore is scheduled for opening in August 1988.

Clearly Scotmid has gone through a considerable process of change. Many of the changes have been of its own making but changes within society have caused Scotmid to re-appraise many of its fundamental values without losing sight of its cooperative origins. The society now looks forward to a period of considerable growth, sure in the knowledge of its sound financial position.

Brewing

Introduction
The brewing and drinking of beer has for generations played an important part in the life and economy of Scotland and, in particular, of Edinburgh. In the West Port, Tollcross and Fountainbridge there were a number of breweries, large and small, which were an important part of industrial life in this area.

Before the Act of Union of 1707, Scotland's drinking habits tended to be centred around wine, port and brandy, particularly from France, with whom Scotland traded under the terms of the so-called 'Auld Alliance'. Only the very poor drank beer, and illicit whisky distilling was widely suppressed. As the terms of the Union were being debated it was rumoured that massive price increases in excise duties on beer were being considered. Angry mobs were seen in Edinburgh outside Parliament, throwing stones and threatening riot. In consequence the Scots Tuppenny Ale retained its pre-Union Excise duty.

After the trade agreement with France had been broken the drinking of beer became more widespread. By the end of the eighteenth century the population of Edinburgh had grown rapidly, increasing both the market for beer and the labour required for the industry: the Maltsmen, Brewers, Copperheadmen, Coopers and Draymen. Although some of the main ingredients of beer had to be imported (sugar and hops), Barley and maize were grown locally in the rich farmlands of East, Mid and West Lothian. Yeast strains were also grown locally, providing unique flavours to the wide variety of beers available in Edinburgh.

The most important ingredient is of course water. Edinburgh is graced with a unique supply of water suitable for brewing beer, for a long time drawn from wells along what has been described as the 'charmed circle' surrounding the city. Large quantities of pure water were easily accessible through the thin layer of sandstone covering the impermeable lava below, caused by a geological fault.

On the west side of the city this fault runs from the Grassmarket to Slateford and a number of breweries took advantage of its water supply. Two such wells were recently uncovered. During building work at Fountainbridge the Fountain well was rediscovered and, during renovations to the King's Theatre, a well was located under the Orchestra pit!

The Early Breweries

Starting at the Grassmarket at the turn of the nineteenth century, there was a large brewery on part of the land previously occupied by the Barras (described in Chapter I), situated at the head of King's Stables Road. It was occupied by George Combe who also owned a Slaughterhouse in that area. Unfortunately nothing else is known about him or his business.

Further up the West Port, between Lady Lawson Street and Lauriston Street, was an establishment thought to be one of the oldest in the area. Its first known owner was Bailie David Rannie, whose gravestone in St Cuthbert's Churchyard showed that he died in 1705. The family name continued with James Rannie who is mentioned in a record of 1755, and Mungo Rannie in a record of 1782. On an improvement plan of 1791 (see Chapter I) evidence of this brewery is apparent, but it may already have closed down. Along its northern perimeter new tenements had been built by this date by James Weir, architect, Alexander Gray, descendant of Robert Gray, Brewer (described below) and a member of the Stein family, thought to be related by marriage to the Haigs of distillery fame.

It is no coincidence that such names appear together. Although brewing was a profitable business during the eighteenth century, but the turn of the next, building was becoming even more profitable. In such a close-knit community of wealthy businessmen it is no surprise that, even in death, their names are linked together. James Weir is buried in David Rannie's tomb alongside Archibald Campbell, Brewer, and his wife Janet Ponton. Janet was the daughter of the architect Alexander Ponton, a contemporary of Weir, whose son Major Weir married Janet's sister Jean.

Further to the north, on the corner of Bread Street and West Port there stood a group of buildings called Hay's court, within which was a small brewery owned by Bailie John Hay. The earliest recording of this brewery was in 1753 but by 1769 it was closed and relocated on the east side of the High Riggs, on the site of Goldberg's Store. Although the evidence is not clear, it is thought that it was later called the Lauriston Brewing Company and, at one time, the Main Point Brewery.

At the beginning of the nineteenth century it is believed that this business was owned by William Wilson, on whose land it was situated. However by 1832 ownership had passed to J P Mitchell who may have been related to the well known merchant of his time Bailie Robert Michel (despite the different spelling) who, in 1726, was described as 'Brewer of Wright's Houses and Portsburgh'. When production at the brewery ceased in 1852 it was under the ownership of the Drumdryan Brewery described next.

Moving on to Leven Street, the Drumdryan Brewery was established in 1760 by Charles Cock. By 1848 James Crease, who was the head brewer of the Main Point Brewery, formed a partnership with James Taylor, which was dissolved in 1856. A new partnership was formed under the name of Taylor, Anderson which was to last until 1870 when the name was changed to Taylor, McLeod until the brewery was demolished in 1905 to make way for the King's Theatre. It is known that Taylor, McLeod used the trademark of a lion rampant, and was famous for its pale, mild ales.

Across the road from the Drumdryan Brewery was Haig's Whisky Distillery, built in 1798 on the site of a much older brewery. This was owned by Robert Gray and built in 1731 on the banks of the Dalry Burn at Lochrin, then described as Newbigging.

Further north on the south side of Morrison Street was a brewery built at the beginning of the eighteenth century. It was entered through a pend to be called Semple's Court, off the north west end of Semple Street. It is described as a large brewery with maltbarns and yards centred around a cobbled yard. In 1758 the premises were seeking a tenant, having previously been owned by G Laidlaw. The brewery was bought by John Semple who, in 1762, was succeeded by his son Robert, who continued with the business until his death in 1819.

Fig 3.3: The coopers of McEwan's Fountain Brewery around 1917.

The Fountain Brewery
William McEwan was born in 1827, the son of a wealthy shipowner and was educated at Alloa Academy. His career began in the offices of the Alloa Coal Company and then in the Glasgow offices of Thomas Lucas Paterson, former owner of the Forth Bank Brewery, who sparked off McEwan's interest in brewing. A second influence on his career came when his sister Janet married James Younger of the Alloa brewing family. Consequently, after a brief spell working in the offices of a spinning mill in Yorkshire, McEwan moved to Edinburgh, determined to learn the brewing trade.

For five years McEwan worked for John Jeffrey at his Heriot Brewery in the Grassmarket, learning the technical and commercial skills of brewing. At the age of twenty-nine and after receiving £2000 from his Younger in-laws, he set out on his own and established the Fountain Brewery at Fountainbridge.

The site chosen for the brewery was well placed on the aforementioned 'charmed circle'. Furthermore, it was close to the Caledonian Railway line, and the Union Canal was only one hundred yards from the Brewery gate. McEwan was quick to take advantage of such good transport facilities and had a railway siding laid directly into the brewery grounds.

Within five years of business, the firm's annual turnover was £40 000, a huge sum in those days. Over half this revenue was gained from the growing markets in the west of Scotland, and substantial profits were made from trade with the north of Scotland and the north of England. Such success was partly due to changes in taste, which had turned from porter to stout to more light bodied pale ales that could quench a thirst. It was also due to McEwan keeping his costs to a minimum by buying malt from other breweries such as the Youngers of Alloa, and by buying bottles and casks from Dryburgh's of Leith, among others. These economies and access to the excellent transport facilities enabled the rapid expansion of the brewery.

No doubt taking advantage of his family's ship-owning connections, his beer was being sent to Australia and New Zealand and, later to India, Canada and South America. Despite initial setbacks, persistence with these markets led the brewery in 1868 to export 250 shipments, worth £34 000. Through such trade, by 1880, the brewery site had expanded to twelve acres.

In 1886 a very prosperous McEwan married Helen Anderson and had a daughter, Margaret. In the same year he was elected to Parliament for Edinburgh Central, standing as a Liberal in favour of Irish Home Rule. He was elected for a further two terms in Parliament but declined to stand again in 1900 for health reasons. To honour his later career in public life and by way of thanks for his gift to the University of the McEwan Hall, he was given the Freedom of the City and an honorary degree. In 1907 he was made a Privy Councillor but, when offered a life peerage, he turned it down. After a long and fruitful life he died at the age of eighty-six at his daughter's home in Surrey in 1913. His daughter did not have children and so the direct McEwan line died with her in 1942.

Meanwhile in 1889 the firm was registered as a limited liability company, with capital estimated at one million. While McEwan was pursuing his career in politics his nephew, William Younger, became Managing Director and prompted further expansion. In 1894 the first maltings were erected at Slateford, followed by a second in 1877. Younger married Katherine Dundas in 1902 and had two sons, the second christened William McEwan Younger, who was later to become Chairman of Scottish Brewers Ltd.

Fortune was not always with the growing company. The war years of 1914–18 proved to be difficult times because of restrictions on raw materials, output and gravity. Overseas trade ceased almost entirely. Because of these setbacks and in an effort to reduce overheads, a merger was announced in 1931 with William Younger and Co, Ltd, of Holyrood (no relation to the Youngers of Alloa). However, although the two original companies pooled many resources, they retained a degree of autonomy.

The Second World War was even more detrimental to the export trade, even though McEwans were a large supplier of beer to the armed forces. Later, as British Colonial power shrank, and as overseas countries developed their own produce, foreign markets went into steep decline, leaving the domestic market the main target for sales. Here, McEwans developed as a hugely successful supplier of bottled beers, Export proving to be one of Britain's most popular beers, appearing in cans in the 1950s as a market leader.

In 1959 a full merger with Youngers resulted in the formation of Scottish Brewers Ltd and, later, Scottish and Newcastle Breweries Ltd.

The optimism of the workforce of the 1950s and 1960s proved to be premature. Scottish and Newcastle had other plans. Modern innovations and advances in technology were to affect the brewing industry as radically as they have influenced other industries.

The old brewery on the north side of Fountainbridge was becoming increasingly obsolete. Plant and working methods were deemed past their day. Processes which had been carried out manually since the early days of brewing were by now regarded as inefficient. A large workforce meant high wage costs and gave the workers inherent power through union organisation. A strike in one department of the brewery could hold up the production throughout the works. In addition limits on the time for the throughput of beer stemmed from a manual pattern of production. By the 1960s the technology was available to circumvent these costly labour intensive methods. In July 1973 the new Fountain Brewery was opened. This new facility had cost Scottish and Newcastle £13 million to build and was then one of the largest and most fully automated brewing complexes in the world. Situated directly opposite the old brewery, which was to be retained as a packaging and distribution centre, on an eleven acre site, previously the home of the North British Rubber Mill, the new complex is flanked by Fountainbridge and the Union Canal.

Two of the fastest and most advanced canning lines in the world, capable of filling 1500 16oz cans per minute, and a huge brewhouse block are housed at this complex. Throughout the negotiations between management and the representatives of the Transport and General Workers Union, management maintained that the new brewery and canning line would mean more employment rather than less, as was feared by the union. The Brewery Management won that argument in the 1970s. Since then more flexible working practices have been initiated and a good many older workers have sought voluntary redundancy. Consequently the present workforce has shrunk to one third of its former size. At a recent vote taken by Transport and General Workers at the brewery, 264 were eligible to vote. Fears that the workforce could decline further now stem from a rumoured plan to establish another canning facility at their Royal Brewery in Manchester. At present fifteen workers on a shift at the canning line are producing 35 000–40 000 cans. Potentially the shift

Fig 3.4: An advertisement for McEwan's Export in the 1950s.

could produce 50 000 cans, so the workers on the line at the old brewery are concerned over their future. Hopefully their fears will prove unfounded.

Distilling

On 30 November 1798 a sasine was granted to James and John Haig for the premises of the old brewery site owned by Robert Gray, situated between modern day Lochrin Place and Terrace. The area covered four acres of ground backing onto the Haig's private basin joined to the Union Canal.

It is thought that John left the business quite early to start up his own distillery but James is known to have remained with Lochrin Distillery until his death in 1833. Both John and James were the sons of John Haig of Gartlands. James had opened his first distillery at Canonmills in 1783 and, against all the odds, made a successful business out of it.

Whisky distilling was not up until then, a 'respectable' trade with which to be involved. The spirit was frowned upon by the upper reaches of society and was identified with the rebellious Highlanders who continued to produce 'illicit' whisky even after the drink had become legal to make under licence.

It was indeed a drink for the masses, as James Haig was fully to appreciate in 1784 when an angry mob invaded his Canonmills Distillery, angry that Haig was supposedly making whisky out of oats and potatoes. Haig faced with the destruction of his building and stills, addressed the crowd in a forthright manner, explained carefully what ingredients were actually used (the correct ones) and eventually pacified the gathering.

Haig rose to become the champion of large-scale 'respectable' distilling. Through his skill of negotiation and foresight, he played a major role in improving prices, duties and excise regulations. Such changes led to the greater profitability of legal spirit production while making it less profitable to produce whisky illegally.

Lochrin Distillery was, at one time, the largest in Scotland and the brand name of Haig is still used by the Distillers Co Ltd. It is not known when production came to a halt at Lochrin but the distillery had certainly closed before 1852. For a while a Paraffin Works used part of the site but new tenements were erected there towards the end of the nineteenth century.

Linen Making

In the early eighteenth century, Alexander Brand of Dalry, feued a portion of land on what is now Grove Street to a linen manufacturer called David Spence. Although the exact date of opening has not been determined, it is known that the business did not last for much more than twenty years. In 1748 the site was put on sale and was described as 'that large factory, dwelling house and garden. The factory measures 108ft long and 19ft broad, being three storeys high'. It would seem that competition from English manufacturers proved to be overwhelming and he went out of business.

Printing

Around 1770 the author and engraver Andrew Bell secured a site on Fountainbridge close to the former linen mill, and had built there a printing works. It was here that the early editions of the *Encyclopaedia Britannica* were printed and which proved to be a great success. Bell was to make a considerable fortune out of this venture which, after publication of the third edition of the volumes, led to sales of over 10 000 copies.

Andrew Bell died in 1809 and his son-in-law Thomson Bonar carried on the printing business until the copyright for the Encyclopaedia was purchased by John Constable and Co, in 1812.

Rope-Making

Prior to the construction of the Union Canal in 1822, there stood a long but low building between modern day Gilmore Place and the eventual course of the Canal. This was the rope-making factory of Samuel Gilmore, who had been brought up in his father and uncle's rope business, and whose son, William, carried on with their retail and wholesale trade in the Grassmarket well into the nineteenth century.

The rope was manufactured and later twisted in a long narrow shed or alley called a 'rope-walk', the great lengths of which were pulled by horse or pony. Although the rope works itself seems to have closed early in the nineteenth century, the rope walk survived until much later. From oral testament it is known that a rope business was still in existence until the 1920s.

Meat Marketing and Tanning

The meat trade was an exceedingly important industry in the area, even until recently. In past ages the needs of the Castle garrison were met and were surpassed by a growing Old and New Town. As an important trade route to the town, Fountainbridge, Tollcross and the West Port, both benefited and suffered from the early growth of cattle and sheep markets at King's Stables Road, the Grassmarket and Wester Portsburgh. As the population increased and older sites became redundant through age and disrepair the new markets of the nineteenth century appeared in Leven Street, Bread Street, the High Riggs and, the largest of them all, in Lauriston.

With the trade in animals came the slaughterhouses, which were often immediately adjacent to one another. The largest in the area before 1850 was the Shambles at King's Stables Road, situated on property owned by Goerge Combe, a Brewer. The allied industry of Tanning was also prolific, found almost exclusively in the West Port even until later in the nineteenth century. In 1852 there were four.

In 1850, however, the Shambles was closed along with all the other smaller slaughterhouses as a result of complaints about the stench and fears

Fig 3.5: A painting of the 'old' slaughterhouse, at King's Stables Road, called 'The Shambles'.

concerning disease (see also Chapter 2). A new municipal slaughterhouse was opened in 1851 between Lochrin distillery and Fountainbridge, which was to remain there until 1912. The dead meat trade continued at Ponton Street and Fountainbridge well into this century, and one company, Swift and Company, remained in the area until 1976.

The Castle Silk Mill

In 1836 an English company was in the process of developing a site on the north side of the canal at Fountainbridge where a large silk spinning mill was to be built. The grounds had been feued from the Governers of the Trades Maiden Hospital at the cost of £100 per annum and an unknown sum paid for rent. The contract to a local builder was to cost around £1100 for the central building and, with further extensions, an engine room and other necessary facilities, the estimated total cost was to reach nearly £4000. Added to this was the need for a steam engine with a capacity of 140 horse power which was installed along with the required silk-making machinery. In total the estimated cost of setting up the mill was in the region of £20 000 which was a very substantial outlay in those days.

Hopes were high in the Burgh that this development would absorb some of Edinburgh's unemployed. Indeed the *Edinburgh Evening Courant* of 13

October 1836 printed an article which maintained confidently that 1500 people would be required to work at the mill, benefiting the local community in particular. However, from the 1841 census returns we find that less than thirty people who lived in or around Fountainbridge were registered as working for the Silk Mill and the vast majority of these were young (20–30 years old) tradesmen from England described as spinners, twisters, reevers, dyers, throwsters and carders.

It would appear that local expectations had been premature. Silk production requires a high degree of skill and experience and it is thought that the company had found it necessary to import these skills from south of the border. However, it is also fairly certain that if the mill had been a successful business it would have required a large workforce of unskilled or semi-skilled workers, easily found in the immediate vicinity.

It is not known exactly when the Mill closed but it had been recorded as being vacant for a number of years before the North British Rubber Company took over the site in 1859. Shortage of skilled labour coupled with competition in the west of Scotland and the eventual decline in the silk-making industry as a whole by 1870 may have been the main factors in its demise, which, considering the cost of the venture, must have been a devastating loss to its owners and a great disappointment to the local community.

Rubber Making

One of the most important employers in our area for five generations was the Castle Mill rubber factory. From a modest beginning in 1856 it grew to be the major source of employment for thousands of families, not only from the area, but also from further afield, so great was the demand for labour. Housed initially in the small building of the old Silk Mill, it grew into a facility covering nearly twenty acres of land on the south side of Fountainbridge.

As it grew in size the presence of the mill became pervasive; the incessant hum of machinery and the smell of rubber in the air was a fact of life. An employee of the Mill was easily identifiable due to his facial pallor and the aroma from his overalls.

The North British Rubber Company was established on the site of the Castle Silk Mill close to the Union Canal. The founder, Henry Lee Norris, a wealthy American, had initially intended to found his factory on the west coast of Scotland but could not find a satisfactory location. However, Edinburgh Corporation, who owned the land, made it more than attractive to Norris by offering it for a peppercorn rent. The ground feu duty for the property was 'two pennies over the price of a pint of ale', a great incentive even in 1856. This, along with other attractions, such as the availability and cheapness of coal tar and lampblack transported easily by canal (also a source of cooling-water) were the deciding factors for Norris.

Having brought four skilled operatives from America—three men and a woman—they immediately set about training local workers in the manufacture of rubber products, initially footwear, such as galoshes. The success

Fig 3.6: Rubber mill workers away from the sweat and smell aboard a specially decorated lorry advertising Keds Casual Wear in 1938.

of the venture can be appreciated by the fact that, within the first twelve years of production, the number of operatives had risen to 600.

Major technological advances of the period stimulated demand for rubber products. For example, a major order for the mill came in 1870 when the need arose for enormous rubber wheels, weighing 750lbs each, for traction engines introduced by R Thompson. In later years the most important development in the demand for rubber manufacturing came with the invention and development of the first detachable pneumatic tyre in 1890 by W E Bartlett, the son-in-law of the founder. The North British Rubber Company was to pioneer many products such as wellingtons, hot water bottles, printers' blankets, and rubber flooring, to name but a few. By 1900 there were two separate production plants, side by side: the North British Rubber Company and the Scottish Vulcanite Company Limited, the former employing 600 people, the latter 500. Vulcanisation was a hardening process applied to rubber to render it suitable for making combs, knife handles and the like.

Demand for rubber goods increased massively in 1914 with the advent of the Great War. Not only had the British army to be supplied by also the allied armies, destined for the mud of the trenches at Ypres and the Somme. Thousands of kits had to be provided; boots, waterproofs and tyres for transport. The Castle Mills design for trench boots was chosen by the Ministry of Defence and at the height of the war it was producing 2750 pairs a day, reaching a total of 1195036 pairs by the end of the carnage. Also supplied to the forces were 70 000 pairs of boots and shoes, 248 326 pairs of gymshoes, 47 000 pairs of heavy snow boots (for the French army alone), 16 103 tyres and 2.5 million feet of hosepipe. Production had to go flat out to meet this phenomenal demand and the mill ran day and night for the four years of the war.

Between the wars the growth of the leisure industry is reflected in products coming off the line at the mill. For example golf-ball production boomed. Casual, rubber-soled shoes called Keds, the precursor of the modern 'trainer' also gained in popularity. However, although production at the mill had to change its emphasis it maintained a large workforce.

During the 1930s, when it was obvious that Germany was once again on a war footing, the mill reverted back to its previous role as major supplier to the forces. At the peak of the Second World War, 80 per cent of the entire output of the factory was war material. As technology advanced, new products had to be developed and produced along with the standard footwear and clothing—inner tubes, anti-gas boots, balloon fabric and millions of gas-masks for the civilian population. The engineering department of the mill was converted to manufacturing machine tools for making aeroplane parts.

After the war the mill reverted once again to the production of peace-time necessities, making everything from combs to coal pit conveyor belts. This production seemed to guarantee the rubber industry and the Mill a healthy future, but this was not to be the case. Twenty years later the mill closed.

Fig 3.7: A view of the North British Rubber Mill after its closure in 1959, showing Mill Lane, now called Gilmore Park.

The tendency of industry in the twentieth century has been for production to aglomerate into the large multi-national companies, the rubber industry being no exception. By the early 1950s fifty per cent of the capital of the North British Rubber Company was held by US Rubber Incorporated. This had increased to seventy-four per cent by the late 1950s although the mill's future on the site seemed safe. Three million pounds had been spent on modernising plant in 1956 and in 1959 a new hose factory was in operation. However, decisions taken overseas were to effect the outcome and in 1965 the remaining ordinary shares were purchased, at £1 each, by a Viennese merchant bank, Schoeller and Company, for a total of £528 353, on the understanding that the Bank would transfer to US Rubber their holding of the shares in exchange for stock of US Rubber.

Then in January 1966 North British Rubber merged with Sto-Chem Ltd to form Uniroyal Ltd. Financial incentives from government agencies proved overwhelming and, by 1966, the plant was re-located at Newbridge in Midlothian. Finally, the tyre combine, Continental, took over Uniroyal at Newbridge in 1979. These deals in international capital were far outwith the influence of the unions and the workforce and was no reflection on their loyalty to the company. Indeed quite a few followed the company to Newbridge to retain their jobs.

The record of the Rubber Mill workforce had been exemplary with no history of long-term disruption of production by strikes. Indeed loyalty was a prominent feature throughout its history. In August 1914 440 men volunteered for the forces and during the course of the war a further 500 joined, of which 160 gave their lives.

Edinburgh's *Evening News* of 8 January 1965 reported that three workers had been presented with gold watches for forty or more years service—Frank Stephen, Jim Ainslie and John Cooper. Their fathers had previously been presented with similar awards. It was not unknown for three generations of a family to work at the 'Mill'. In the locality the mill was more a way of life than a mere job.

Further reading

1 An Onlooker, (1911). *Edinburgh Street Studies.*
2 Dunlop, A H, (1890). *Anent Old Edinburgh.*
3 St Cuthbert's Cooperative Association, (1959). *One Hundred Years of Cooperation.*

4

Transport

Jean Redgers

Introduction

Before Lothian Road was built in 1788 three of the most important roads in the City passed through Tollcross. When the New Town was built the significance of these roads was overshadowed by the developing communications of a growing city and the complexity of the industrial age. Over the next one hundred years these developments transformed Tollcross into one of the most important transport junctions in Edinburgh.

Canal transport was slow to reach Edinburgh. Early attempts to forge a canalway into the centre of Georgian Edinburgh were impractical and against public interest. By the time the Union Canal was built in 1822 into Fountainbridge from Falkirk and Glasgow, the early railways were being conceived. Although the canal survived until 1922 its importance was easily surpassed by the growth of the railway.

However, the Union Canal brought with it the need for improved roads to cope with the incoming industries in Fountainbridge. The influx of canal and industrial workers meant a dramatic rise in population and its consequent poor living conditions.

The expansion of the railway into the Lothian Road area and its cut-throat competiton for access to the City and to Leith speeded up the process of industrial and population growth in the latter half of the nineteenth century which added to the congestion and vibrancy of the Tollcross area.

As road networks improved throughout the City towards the end of last century, Tollcross became the important road junction it is today with its familiar six-spoked crossroads. For horsedrawn, cable and electric trams as well as buses, Tollcross was an ideal place to site a depot—built in West Tollcross—sharing with Shrubhill the transport needs of a city at least half the size it is today.

Little has changed of the shape of the Tollcross area but the canal has all but gone, the railway is now a roadway and traffic congestion is problematic. A population decimated by the decline in local industry, by the ravages of demolition, and the lure of supposedly better housing in the outlying schemes, is now faced with a conflict of interests with the needs of commuters from the better off suburbs of the city.

Fig 4.1: The Union Canal in the early 1820s, looking towards the Castle. The wooden bridge carried Semple Street over the canal and on the other side of the bridge was Port Hopetoun. The tenement to the left of the bridge was the first to be built on Bread Street. The one on the right is 163 Lothian Road. Both are still standing.

Canal Transport

In the late eighteenth century, as the Industrial Revolution gathered pace, a cheaper and quicker way of supplying coal to Edinburgh was being discussed by pit owners and coal suppliers in the city. Up to the beginning of the new century, although some of this coal came from local fields (especially East and Midlothian), the bulk of it came from Alloa, Wemyss and Newcastle by sea, which was very expensive and attracted a 3s 6d per ton duty. It was also too expensive to bring large supplies over land from coalfields in the west. Consequently in January 1793, a group of interested gentlemen met to discuss the idea of building a canal to link West Lothian and Lanarkshire with Edinburgh.

Discussions were initiated with the landowners concerned on the most suitable route the canal would take, and the businessmen who would need wharfs for the easy loading and unloading of their goods.

In 1797 various routes connecting Leith with the Clyde were surveyed and reported by a number of engineers. All the plans were submitted to an engineer from London, Mr Rennie, for his opinion. Rennie reported that none of these routes would satisfy objections and, as an alternative, he suggested a route from Hillhead, Glasgow, by way of Cumbernauld and Falkirk to a basin at Bruntsfield Links above Wright's Houses. A series of locks would then take the canal down to a terminus at the east end of the Meadows. However, objections were again raised and certain modifications were made to accommodate a new route via Cleland, Midcalder and Ratho, although the Edinburgh connection was still in dispute.

Along with these disagreements were the aggravating consequences of the European war with France, so it was not until 1813 that the question of the Edinburgh canal route was readdressed, with more surveys requested and different routes presented. By this time the Forth and Clyde canal had been built. A proposal was tendered by Mr Hugh Baird, engineer in charge of building that canal to take a branch from Lock 16 of the Forth and Clyde at Falkirk into Edinburgh, by way of Fountainbridge. The proposed basin was at Lochrin, adjacent to John and James Haig's Distillery, and two extensions would take the canal further into the centre of the city. The first would cut across Ponton Street and Thornybauk, and continue across the heart of Tollcross, terminating at the east end of the Meadows. The second would run from a basin at the head of Lothian Road by a series of locks to nearly the foot of that road, traversing it to bypass St Cuthbert's Church into what is now Princes Street Gardens, to the Waverley Market. (Previous plans had also chosen the Waverley site and, in anticipation of events, a street in the vicinity was named Canal Street.)

Baird estimated that the cost of this route into Edinburgh would be £235 167, offset by an annual revenue of £20 000 from coal, £11 750 from lime, £3000 from passage boats, £625 from building stone and £500 from iron and timber. His estimate was immediately attacked by the landowners as too low and they were angry at the proposed buying price of only £122 per acre of their land.

In April of 1814 the Edinburgh Magistrates announced that they would oppose the coming Union Canal Bill going through Parliament accepting Baird's route. Their biggest objection was the use of the Meadows as a Canal Basin, saying that a route to Leith would be more favourable. Robert Stevenson (grandfather of Robert Louis Stevenson) was invited to report on such a plan. Given this opposition, in October of that year, Baird increased his estimate by about £10 000 and dropped the plans for the Meadows branch. Stevenson countered with a further plan to bring a canal up from Leith to the now drained North Loch (Princes Street Gardens) to creat an elaborate inner city loch, with the intention of forming an ornamental beauty spot in the heart of Edinburgh.

By 1815 all the arguments had been made and costs discussed. All question of a link with Leith was seen financially to be unsound and most of Baird's route agreed to be the best tender. The Union Canal Committee further approached Thomas Telford, who gave his approval, and the Union Canal Bill of 1817 was put into motion. Both the Meadows and the North Loch routes were abandoned, and the final decision to terminate the Canal at Lothian Road was secured.

In that year a new Committee was elected and Mr Robert Downie of Appin was elected Chairman and later, President, of the Company. On 3 March 1818, on the site of what was to become the Port Hopetoun basin at Lothian Road, after a short prayer by a minister from St Cuthbert's Parish, Mr Downie dug the first spadeful of earth amid cheers from the onlookers, to commemorate the start of the Edinburgh end of the canal. Mr Downie declared that it was one of the proudest and happiest days of his life.

During the building of the canal, labour was plentiful. Owing to unemployment and poverty at home many Highlanders and Irishmen were recruited along with local men to work as 'navvies', the name given to Navigational Canal Workers. These migrant workers were reputedly of a rowdy nature, but distance from home and family and their 'foreign' nature may have contributed to the attitudes of the workforce. Religious bigotry may also have played a part, especially against the Catholic Irish.

Although they worked hard over long hours, they always took great pride in their appearance. Their distinctive clothes consisted of a white felt hat or peaked cap, a red spotted handkerchief (worn around the neck and tied in a knot), a brightly coloured shirt, a waistcoat, moleskin trousers, with leather overboots completing the rig-out.

Two of the Irishmen, William Burke and William Hare, met while working on the canal as navvies and are better known as the infamous partnership (adding murder to their canal duties) who provided bodies for medical research at the Royal Infirmary. Burke was hanged for his crimes but Hare turned King's evidence and was pardoned.

Work progressed well along the canal and, after completion in May 1822 at a cost of £40 000 (well in excess of the original estimate!), there were three basins in the Fountainbridge area: Port Hopetoun (between the Carron Cinema and Semple Street), Port Hamilton (latterly St Cuthbert's Bakery, Dairy and Transport section), and Lochrin (behind Gilmore Place), which was a private basin used by Haig's Distillery. The canal passed over Fountainbridge under the iron lifting bridge, now at Gilmore Park, and over Semple Street beneath a wooden bridge.

In that year the first passage boat was launched—the Flora McIvor—built in Lochrin, behind Gilmore Place. The second boat, the Di Vernon (like the Flora McIvor, named after a character from Walter Scott's novels), was launched later that year, and the Appin, Munro and Union followed later.

Port Hopetoun, named after the Earl of Hopetoun, whose coalfields supplied much of the canal's coal haulage, was the largest of the basins, stretching from Morrison Street, nearly to Fountainbridge. At the west end of the basin was a three storeyed house reputed to belong to the Earl of Hopetoun. On the top floor was the home of the Canal Superintendent, the second floor the Canal Office and on the first a tile merchant. A converted dovecot standing nearby functioned as a ticket office for the three daily services, at 7.00 am, 2.00 pm and 6.00 pm. The passenger fare to Glasgow was 6s 6d for a cabin, or 4s 6d for less comfortable accommodation on deck. Services were also advertised from Edinburgh to America on this route, sailing from Glasgow. Excursion trips to Ratho and the Almond Aqueduct also became popular in the 1830s, costing 6d a seat.

Building work round Hopetoun increased rapidly, including warehouses, stables and an Inn. A large terminal building was erected on the landing square for passengers. there was also a boat building yard. Apart from passenger and coal transport, the Port handled lime, stone, iron, bricks and other merchandise.

Fig 4.2: The iron drawbridge which took Fountainbridge over the canal before the bridge was removed in 1920 to its current location across Gilmore Park at the Lochrin Basin.

Port Hamilton was situated between Gardner's Crescent and Semple Street and was built in 1823 as a coal basin. Along its sides were stored the vast amounts of coal being transported from the Duke of Hamilton's coalfields at Redding and Brighton, as well as from those belonging to the Earl of Hopetoun.

By the 1830s competition for rail transport had started to threaten canal transport. To the south of Edinburgh the Lothian coalfields were taking advantage of the developing Edinburgh–Dalkeith railway, partly horse-operated from Craighall to St Leonard's. At this time three bills were put forward to build a railway line from Edinburgh to Glasgow but naturally were opposed by the Union Canal Company and were temporarily shelved. However, by 1838, although still heavily opposed by the Company, a Bill was passed through Parliament to allow the Edinburgh and Glasgow (E & G) Railway Company a line, opening in 1842.

Consequently the Union Canal Company reduced their fares and duties, which the railway company duly matched. By 1845 the Company began to lose money and was taken over by the Forth and Clyde canal in an attempt to rationalise the service. However, in 1849 it too was taken over by the Edinburgh and Glasgow Railway Company and decline set in. In 1865 the growing North British Railway Company bought over the E & G and their canal interests and, after unsuccessful attempts to promote trade the canal went further into decline. Revenue figures for the next fifty years tell the whole story:

1870 £5209
1900 £3267
1907 £2381
1921 £1169

By 1922 Ports Hopetoun and Hamilton were finally closed and a year later the canal passed to the London and North Eastern Railway, who swallowed up the North British Railway. The Ports were sold to the Corporation of Edinburgh. In the early 1920s all commercial traffic to Edinburgh had ceased and the canal was drained and filled in from Lochrin. The bridge across Fountainbridge was removed and repositioned at Gilmore Park, although no longer functioning as a lifting bridge. The buildings were demolished and the rubble used for in-filling.

The Port Hopetoun site lay derelict until 1936 when a new building called Somerset House was built. Public opinion was immediately set against the English name and Lothian House was substituted. On the ground floor, as now, there were shops, and the above three floors were occupied by the Inland Revenue Department. In 1938 the Regal Cinema was added, to become the ABC and now the Cannon Film Centre. On the front elevation of Lothian House there is a sculpture set into the wall, commemorating the Basin. Designed by Pilkington Jackson, it depicts a canal barge with horse and outrider, with the inscription: 'Here stood Port Hopetoun 1822–1922'.

Port Hamilton was developed earlier and was taken over by St Cuthbert's Cooperative Society (now Scotmid) in 1925, housing a large bakery and milk depot.

Although commercial traffic ceased in the 1930s, the remaining stretch of the canal along Fountainbridge was still an important source of water for local industries, such as the North British Rubber Company. Each week about twenty-eight million gallons of water were provided. However, apart from being a water supply it had no other use except for pleasure boating which, in the stretch of canal from Craiglockhart to Fountainbridge, was hardly advisable and, given the pollution and dumping of rubbish, was for decades, literally a backwater.

In 1955 a campaign to close the canal was initiated by local people fearing their children's safety, and 3000 signatures were submitted to Edinburgh Corporation. Three years later the Corporation agreed that no further commercial interests were conceivable but it was not until 1963 that the canal was formally closed, despite the fact that no plans were carried out to make it safe or fill it in. In fact it became an unofficial dumping ground for rubbish of all description.

During the late 1960s, and for the next decade, people with various opinions discussed the problems of the canal and what should be done with it. Gradually, interested parties began to see the potential for sport and leisure, and many individuals and environmental groups gave their time to cleaning the canal.

Boating has been popular on the canal for a number of years and several schools and clubs still own boathouses along the city stretches. Indeed school pupils were prominent in clearing the Harrison Park to the Slateford Aqueduct section. One of the oldest boathouses has been run by the St Andrew's Club at Meggetland since 1846. The Forth Canoeing Club still make good use of the Lochrin stretch where the canal terminates behind Scottish and Newcastle Brewery.

Once the canal had been cleaned fishing improved, with a growing number of roach, pike, perch and eel coming back to these waters. The author notes that this is a far cry from the days between the wars when boys armed with a jam jar and net, fished in the canal for minnows!

The Union Canal is now managed by the British Waterways Board who employ a Countryside Ranger, based at Broxburn, giving advice on all canal activities. From Fountainbridge to Falkirk there are many developed stretches of the canal, suitable for walkers and nature lovers. A great variety of plant and bird life now proliferate the canal side. Many people are now aware of the countryside only a short walk from Tollcross.

In 1986 the Edinburgh Canal Society was formed to further the use of the canal by the community for sport and leisure. Several proposals have also been made by commercial enterprise to develop the Fountainbridge end of the Canal with floating restaurants and other leisure pursuits. Over the next decade important decisions regarding the future will no doubt show up conflicts of interest between environmentalists and commerce, but for the moment, although its original use is now history, if Robert Downie were here today he would be proud of the tremendous enthusiasm and effort that has gone into making the canal the well-preserved and appreciated waterway it is now.

Rail Transport

As described in the last section, the growing transport needs of the late eighteenth and early nineteenth centuries saw town merchants taking advantage of developing canal communications, even although they were slow, expensive and could not carry the large volume of goods in demand, especially coal.

In 1824 plans were laid out to build Edinburgh's first railway (the Edinburgh and Dalkeith (E & D)), used to bring coal from the Midlothian coalfields at a time when it was scarce and expensive to transport by road and sea. By the 1830s the E & D was carrying three hundred tons a day. Soon, new railways began to be discussed with the coal lords. There was much agreement about the greater viability of rail transport but, when it came to defining routes, once again there was disagreement because each pit owner naturally wanted rails to run beside his own pit. There were delays, and problems too, trying to fix prices with landlords for the sale of land on which to lay the tracks and for the minerals which lay under them.

By the 1840s many of the disagreements had been solved and a network of railways reached most of the coal pits in the Forth and Clyde valley, now competing more successfully with the Lothian pits and English coal.

Although coal was the motivating factor in the early days of rail transport, in 1836 a railway was built to accommodate passengers as well as goods, through the Midlands to the north, by Preston. Railway engineer Joseph Locke was then to survey a route to carry the railway to Carlisle and hence to Glasgow and Edinburgh. However, difficulties were ahead because of the nature of the terrain, often unsuitable for locomotives.

After pressure from J J Johnstone MP, who had an early involvement with the railway, Locke accepted a route through Annandale (a large estate of which was owned by Johnstone) principally because it cut the journey to Edinburgh by twenty miles and to Glasgow by fifty miles, as compared to the Nithsdale route previously considered. Although this great Scottish undertaking was financed mainly by English funds, it was to be controlled by Scottish interests and appropriately called the Caledonian Railway Company.

The Caledonian Railway was opened on 15 February 1848, from Carlisle to Glasgow and the Carstairs to Edinburgh branch was opened two months later. The route was eight miles longer than the Edinburgh and Glasgow Railway Company's line, opened in 1842, with a terminus at Haymarket, but the Caledonian ran trains four times a day each way. Fearing competition, the E & G had bought the Union Canal in 1845 for £209 000 in an attempt to increase their transport revenues, but more especially to thwart attempts by the Caledonian to drain the canal, using its bed for the new line.

The E & G also reduced fares drastically and the Caledonian followed suit, nearly ruining both companies, before the Caledonian could even begin to develop its service. Now in deep financial difficulties, caused partly by bad management and partly by competition forced by the E & G, and with share prices falling and shareholders rightly very angry, things looked very gloomy indeed for the new company. It must have come as a great surprise and a greater relief when John Baird, a rich iron merchant, walked confidently into the Company's Head Office in Edinburgh and invested a large sum of money. Luckily too, most of the Company's Board members retired and the Caledonian came into its own.

Competition loomed from another quarter however, with the authorisation of the North British Railway (NBR) in 1844. Both companies (as well as the smaller E & G) were set on monopolising the rail link to the centre of the city and forging the best route connecting the city with the port of Leith. The NBR had managed to open the North Bridge Station (Waverley) by June of 1846, and the E & G joined them there two months later.

Once formed, the Caledonian also planned to build a (grand) terminal station in Edinburgh as the Company Headquarters. The station at Lothian Road was designated with a classical façade, some 370 feet in length and, as one member of the Board stated, it would be a greater station than any in London.

The Duke of Atholl laid the foundation stone for the new station on 9 April 1847. The Duke, who was the Grand Master of the Freemasons at the time, was accompanied by other officials of the Grand Lodge, the Lord Provost, City Magistrates and the Board members of the Railway Company. There were many speeches and much pomp and ceremony, but all was to no avail; the fine promises were empty, owing to the financial mess the company had endured. Nothing further was added to the foundation which in no way met expectations. A year later, in place of the grand building was a shack-like wooden structure.

This building, called Lothian Road Station, was only 180 feet long and 54 feet wide, and was built close to St Cuthbert's Workhouse, where the Sheraton

Fig 4.3: The second of three Caledonian Railway Company stations in the vicinity of the Lothian Road. It was called Princes Street Station, and was built in 1870. It was destroyed by fire in 1890.

Hotel and the head of the Western Approach Road now exist. It was considered to be a disgrace to the capital and stood for twenty-two years until the Workhouse was demolished in 1870, allowing expansion closer to Princes Street.

In 1870 came another new station building, again a wooden structure but much larger. It displaced both the Workhouse and the former Kirk Brae House, which stood at the corner of Lothian Road and Rutland Street, and remained there for the next twenty years.

In 1890 a fire swept through the greater part of Princes Street Station, as it was known, which luckily had been heavily insured. Part of the building was saved and used for goods transport until 1939 when, again, fire destroyed it completely.

With the first insurance returns and its growing profits, the company was now in a position to build a more grandiose station, built of red sandstone and to a wedge-shaped design to fit the shape of the roads at the West End.

The interior was spacious and the narrow entrance opened into a large foreground, ideal for cabs to pick up and deposit passengers. Passengers had easy access on foot because, unlike the Waverley, Princes Street Station was on the street level, so that passengers did not have to descend gloomy steps or windy carriage ramps. It came into operation in 1893 with glass fronted shops and a restaurant. The author recalls how at Christmas time children would crowd in to watch the *model* railway display that was laid out in front of the station platforms. The Hotel above was not added until 1903 but it is now all that remains of this monument to Victorian Railway splendour.

Behind the Caldeonian Station was a large goods depot. Freight was unloaded and distributed by way of Lothian Road. The Parcels and Goods offices still remain at this point. An extensive coal depot was also located at the rear of the main station. The locomotives, though, were housed in the Dalry sheds, bordered by Dundee Street and the locally named 'Coffin Lane'.

Apart from the Caledonian Hotel the only other reminder of the station and goods yard is a wrought iron archway on the right of the Hotel which remains standing, next to the public house aptly called 'Platform One'.

During this period many changes had taken place in railway transport. It had become a way of life and attracted a great deal of public interest and marvel (as well as disapproval!). Great races were fought between rival railway companies, in particular between the Caledonian and the NBR. In 1888, for example, a race from London to Edinburgh was staged, which became one of the highlights of the pageantry of rail travel, and which ignored timetables and virtually all sense of public safety. The east coast route to the Waverley (NBR) won the day, achieving a time of 7 hours 27 minutes, over the west coast Caledonian rivals, who arrived at Princes Street Station 11 minutes later.

Of the Caledonian locomotives, one of the most successful was the 'Dunalister', named after the Company Chairman's home in Perthshire. It was designed by J F McIntosh, who had worked his way up from the engine sheds, and it was one of the most popular and fastest (60 mph) of its day. During

Queen Victoria's Jubilee year of 1897, locomotives 723 and 724 were named Victoria and Jubilee respectively. Just before he retired, Mr McIntosh was made a member of the Royal Victorian Order in recognition of his services to locomotive engineering.

Local transport had been developing too, especially in the link between Edinburgh and Leith, whose docks expanded increasingly in the latter half of the nineteenth century. Amid much the same controversy which had dogged the advancement of canal travel, domination of the city centre lines was also a crucial issue.

As early as 1847 the Edinburgh, Leith and Granton Railway had opened from Canal Street Station (the Waverley Market site) under the New Town by tunnel to Scotland Street and Canonmills. It was an impractical arrangement because of the steep incline involved, as the trains needed to be winched up and down. It closed in 1868 in the same year that the NBR opened its spur to Leith from Waverley. However, the Caledonian had opened its line from Leith, via Granton Road, Craigleith and Dalry Road to Princes Street two years earlier, although it did not carry passengers until 1879.

The two companies were thus locked into stiff competition and were subject to much criticism and lampooning by public and press for their seeming disregard of amenity in favour of profit. However, local transport had improved steadily and, although the issue of railway lines through the centre of Edinburgh was highly contentious, those in the suburbs were benefiting for example from the Edinburgh Suburban and Southside Junction, built in 1884, which ran from Waverley by way of Gorgie, Morningside, Duddingston, and returning to Waverley from the east (a line which still exists today). The NBR here had the advantage of running directly through the city, which the Caledonian also wanted to do, especially to link with the NBR track from Waverley to connect with their own Leith line, thereby forming a northern loop back to Princes Street Station.

By the 1890s the volume of rail traffic had increased enormously and the NBR were planning to extend the Waverley and to lay more lines through Princes Street Gardens. At the same time the Caledonian, ever more anxious to link with the Waverley, proposed a tunnel under Princes Street, with air vents heading on to the Gardens. Public outcry against such an undertaking was acute and, in a desperate attempt to save the day, the Town Council gave permission for the NBR to build another double line through the Gardens. The Caledonian were never to get another chance to expand.

Despite this cut-throat history, both companies were in sound financial condition. The Caledonian had improved its success when the Post Office transferred mail transportation from the east to the west coast line in 1855. The Company's capital in 1887 now stood at £41m and they employed nearly 15000 men. By 1910 it was at the height of its fortunes and carried a staggering 34 million passengers a year and had nearly 1000 locomotives.

In 1923 the Caledonian joined the London, Midland and Scottish Railway Company and, in the same year, the North British merged with the London and North Eastern Railway, thereby increasing their profitability. Both were nationalised into British Rail in 1948.

After the Second World War railway transport slid into gradual decline and the Caledonian Station was an eventual casualty. Private car ownership increased along with advances in tramways and bus transport, which began to expand beyond, and were more flexible than local railway networks. By the early 1960s the fate of many of the nationalised British Rail lines was sealed when Dr Beeching made his very unpopular closures of a huge number of uneconomic lines. In 1962 both the Caledonian's Leith line and the former NBR Suburban line were closed.

The Caledonian Station was finally closed in 1965 as it could no longer compete with the Waverley in terms of routes and accessibility. It was also felt that closing the station would ease traffic problems at the West End. Once the rails were removed the railway line was eventually turned into the Western Approach Road, for the relief of traffic through Gorgie and Dalry. A temporary car park now covers the station grounds.

On 7 August 1973, during road alignment, where the Western Approach Road joins Lothian Road, an interesting discovery was made by the driver of a bulldozer working on the site. The Foundation stone which had been laid by the Duke of Atholl on 9 April 1847 for the building of the first of the Caledonian's stations, was uncovered. Unfortunately a copper plate from the top of the stone, detailing the grand ceremony and those present, was badly damaged. However, a glass jar containing maps, a number of newspapers of the time, Railway reports, and a complete set of coins minted that year (kept in perfect condition by beeswax), had been saved, and are now in the safe-keeping of Huntly House Museum.

Fig 4.4: Contents of the 'Time Capsule' unearthed during road works at the Western Approach Road in 1973. It was originally placed below the foundation stone of the first Caledonian Railway Company station.

The spirit of the Caledonian would seem to have lived on. The now clean red sandstone Caledonian Hotel is now one of Edinburgh's best, and millions of city visitors and residents have observed the smartly dressed Commissionaire, perhaps without realising the bright blue colour of his uniform was used on the Caledonian coaches so many years ago.

Road Transport

The development of road transport in Edinburgh gathered pace during the latter half of the nineteenth century. By the 1880s rail transport had revolutionised long distance travel and had gone some way towards the needs of the city suburbs' dweller. As the city grew it became increasingly difficult to build new rail lines and therefore road transport became ever more crucial.

Since 1610, when Henry Anderson was licensed to run a coach from Edinburgh to Leith, until the turn of the twentieth century, public road transport had relied on the horse. Mechanised road transport did not appear in Edinburgh until 1893 and, even then, problems with hills meant that horses were still needed well into the new century. Indeed the last horse-drawn bus with a terminus at Tollcross lasted until 1907.

Andrew Patterson, describing in 1960 his childhood at the turn of the century, recollected the great number of horses on the streets and the slow cable cars, unable to take the hill at Bruntsfield Links:

> In front of the Barclay Church stood youths, each with a horse. A tramcar, proceeding south, stopped at Glengyle Terrace and a trace-boy (as he was called) yoked his horse to the car to help to pull it up Bruntsfield Place, unyoked it at Leamington Terrace, and seated on its rump, and with a great jangling of chains, gaily cantered down the hill. Sometimes, as a diversion, he didn't return immediately but waited till the next boy came up, and then raced each other back to the Barclay Church.

Street tramways first appeared in 1871 after the Transport Act of the previous year. Before the first rails were built, John Croall had been running an omnibus on a circular route from Tollcross to Morningside and John Atkinson to Morningside Asylum at three pence inside and two pence on top. These buses, however, did not start until 9 or 10 o'clock in the morning and therefore did not suit working people, even if they could afford the expensive fares. In fact, to be seen on horse transport of any description in those days was an indication of higher social standing.

On 29 June 1871 the Edinburgh Street Tramways Company was formed and first rails laid from the West End, by way of Tollcross, to Churchill and from Tollcross to St Giles Cathedral by way of Lauriston Place. The trams, pulled by two horses, could take twelve passengers inside and fourteen in the open top deck. An extra horse had to be hitched up by 'trace boys' on the hill up the High Street to George IV Bridge. The drivers, muffled up against the cold in winter, and working anything up to sixteen hours a day, had to whistle to warn other traffic and pedestrians as they proceeded at a quick walking pace!

Complaints against the tramways were numerous, especially over the

Fig 4.5: Edinburgh and District Tramways Company Car No 72 at the Tollcross terminus on the Colinton Road route just before closure in 1907.

occasional wreckless driver. Animal lovers sympathised with the overworked horses, whose average working life on the trams was four years, after which they were sold at John Croall's Horse Bazaar at the corner of Lady Lawson Street and Castle Terrace. Shoppers also complained that, in places, the lines were so close to the pavement they could not park their own vehicles!

Competition from horse drawn buses was still in evidence until the turn of the century. In 1878 the Tramway Company had contracted a bus company to run a route between Tynecastle Toll and the High Street, by way of Morrison Street and Lauriston, and by 1881 they started their own bus routes. However, by 1904 only two of its local routes remained and, as we have seen, the last horse bus ran in 1907.

It had been obvious for a number of years that horse transport of any sort was becoming obsolete, although a local alternative to the steam engine was not commercially viable or socially acceptable. However, in 1893 a trial cable drawn system was introduced, using steam driven engines at planned local power stations. In this way trams became mechanised for the first time.

The Tollcross Power Station, one of four in the city, was built in 1896 at West Tollcross, where the new Fire Station now stands. Containing four boilers and three pairs of engines drawing five cables, it helped to power the first passenger-paying route from Pilrig, through Tollcross to the Braids, opened in October 1899 by the Edinburgh District Tramway Company. Unfortunately though, during the first runs, a break in the cable, caused by the driver failing to release the gripper on the moving cable, brought the whole system to a full stop. Such accidents happened regularly and, even by 1919, it is reckoned that on average a cable broke once a day.

The public tended to remember the cable cars in terms of their unreliability long after they were replaced by electric versions. Music Hall stories and jokes also recalled boys tying tin cans to the cable, and the drunk man who guided himself home by hooking his walking stick to the cable, only to find he had gone in the wrong direction and was even further from home than he had thought!

Meanwhile Edinburgh Corporation had appreciated the need to develop the motor bus. However they had perhaps been put off by the early liquidation in 1907 of Norman MacDonald's Edinburgh Motor Omnibus Company, which in 1906 had run a Craiglockhart Station, Tollcross, Melville Drive service, using open top, acetylene driven double deckers. In 1906 too the Scottish Motor Traction Company had started a short lived Waverley to Colinton Road service, but which later bought premises in Lauriston Place (later to become the Tollcross Cinema) and by 1911 they had built a larger workshop in East Fountainbridge, expanding to a second bus body building works in Valleyfield Street (now a carpet shop) in 1913. SMT became one of the most successful companies in the Tollcross area, in addition to which their car showrooms at Lothian Road and Morrison Street are well remembered.

In 1914 the Corporation at last allowed the Edinburgh District Tramway Company to run six motor buses on a circular route by way of Tollcross. They were garaged at the Tollcross Tram Depot for a while but were soon commandeered by the War Office. It wasn't until 1919 that the Corporation took on motor bus transport for themselves, with the introduction of the No 1 bus, running from Ardmillan, through Fountainbridge to the Canongate. In 1921 bus transport through Tollcross was increased by the Goldenacre to Bruntsfield route, and then by the Cameron Toll route through Lady Lawson Street and Morrison Street to Haymarket.

Meanwhile, in 1919 the Corporation introduced electric trams and consequently took over the Edinburgh District Tramway Company. In 1923 the West End to Marchmont route was opened, running through Tollcross. Electrification had been achieved despite strong resistance by amenity and motoring lobbies, who predicted correctly that the electric tramway system would virtually monopolise public road transport, complete with its dangerous deep rails and ugly overhead electric cables.

Tollcross Power Station was subsequently closed and converted into an electricity sub-station and depot. The entrance was moved further to the east to accommodate a line from West Tollcross, creating a circular access with Thornybauk to the crossroads and, through this expansion, became one of the most important transport features of the area.

Trams by now had become by far the major carrier of passengers, in spite of competition from the early motor buses, which were not to become prominent until after the Second World War. Trams were also cheap. In 1930 the maximum fare was three pence but nearly seventy per cent of passengers paid the one penny fare. The author recalls the pre-printed tickets punched by the conductor according to the appropriate stages, but which went out of use in 1937 after the introduction in 1933 of the automatic printing ticket machine—TIMS, as it was affectionally called.

Although city buses were slow to take over from trams, there were developments in the out of town services, to be found not far from Tollcross. In 1924, Castle Terrace became a busy bus terminal, firstly with the service to West Linton through Morningside, run by Andrew Harper of Peebles. By 1932 the colourful red and white buses of the Caledonian Omnibus Company also ran to West Linton and as far as Dumfries. The Caledonian's offices were situated at 5 Castle Terrace and it operated there until 1950.

Robert Wilson of Carnwath also ran small Bedford buses from Castle Terrace by way of Fountainbridge to Tarbrax and to Forth on the North Pentlands from 1945 to the early 1960s. His was the only private operator in Edinburgh to obtain a licence after the 1931 Road Traffic Act, and his buses proved popular with weekend fishermen and hill walkers.

In the early 1950s, prolonged discussions took place regarding scrapping tramways in favour of bus transport, which by then had become more commercially viable and a much more flexible alternative. However, opposition to scrapping the trams, which had served the population of Edinburgh well for over thirty years, was surprisingly strong. Indeed in 1952 a Town Councillor in Dalry, who favoured the proposal to do away with trams, lost his seat over this issue.

The arguments continued until 1956 when the Corporation finally closed the curtain on tram transport which, they agreed, had become an outdated, rundown, and uncomfortable form of transport. On 16 November 1956 the final day came and many thousands of people turned out to cheer the 'last tram' ceremony running from Morningside through Tollcross. A great era of transport had eventually come to an end.

Tollcross Tram depot was retained as a bus depot for a while but a new garage at Longstone built in the early 1960s serviced all the needs of a growing service on the west side of the town. Sadly the Tollcross building was demolished and remained a temporary car park for a number of years until the Fire Station was built in 1986 to replace the eighty-year-old building in Lauriston Place.

Further reading

1 Hunter, DGL, (1964). *Edinburgh's Transport.*
2 Lindsay, Jean, (1968). *The Canals of Scotland.*
3 Massey, Alison, (1983). *The Edinburgh and Glasgow Union Canal.*
4 Nock, OS, (1973). *The Caledonian Railway.*
5 Patterson, Andrew, (1966). *Tollcross to Morningside in the Olden Days.*
6 Thomas, John, (1971). *A Regional History of the Railways of Great Britain—Volume 6, Scotland—the Lowlands and the Borders.*

5

At Leisure

Mary MacDonald

Introduction

The story of entertainment in Tollcross is a complex one. Fashions in entertainment changed over the years, and there were consequent changes in the
use or management of the various entertainment centres.

Entertainment, we can be sure, has been provided wherever there are
people to enjoy it. A complete history of it in our area would certainly go
back at least as far as the jousting which took place in mediaeval times on
the barras or jousting ground adjoining the site of King's Stables Road.
However, to make the theme more manageable the story here starts from the
early nineteenth century when the area was becoming populous.

Circuses and fairs were the principal sources of amusement. The circus
business started by Thomas Cooke (to be described in more detail later) started
in 1835 and flourished till 1911. There were also travelling shows held on
open spaces in the area. The first theatre to be built, in 1875, was the West
End Theatre, later to become the Synod Hall. It failed, apparently because of
poor management, but the Lyceum Theatre opened in 1883 and soon became
a continuing success. This was the era of the great actor-managers who, with
their touring companies, were much improving the standard of theatrical
entertainment outside London. The New Pavilion Theatre in Grove Street,
later to become a cinema, opened in 1897, and the King's Theatre in 1906.

As to concerts, Tollcross does not enter the scene until 1914, but then does
so in a very big way with the opening of the Usher Hall.

However, the greatest developments were to come from the magic lantern
and tent shows given on fairgrounds. An early example of the former was
situated in Lothian Road where an impressive building housed exhibitions of
light shows reflecting pictures with mirrors and lenses, called a Diorama. In
the same building one could see a similar exhibition of views of different parts
of the world called a Cosmorama. From these came the 'penny geggies' which
were different to the static exhibitions in that they used devices which gave
the illusion of movement. From these developed the cinema. Many of the
early cinema proprietors were descended from the travelling showmen, and
of these probably the Poole family made the biggest impact on the cinema
both in Edinburgh as a whole and in Tollcross.

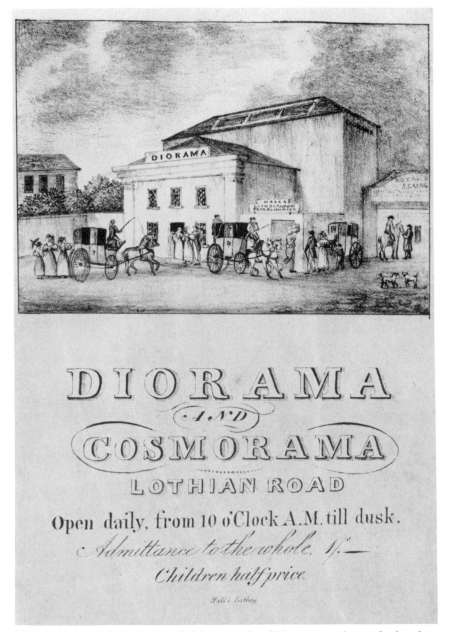

Fig 5.1: The early light shows called 'Dioramas' and 'Cosmoramas' were displayed in this building on Lothian Road near to where the Caledonian Hotel now stands. The drawing is dated 1834 and also shows the Royal Academy for Teaching Exercises (see Chapter 6).

The early patrons, at the beginning of the present century, were working class people in crowded areas such as Tollcross. The accommodation was makeshift—even a circus ring was pressed into use. The Central Halls (described in more detail in the chapter on churches) was another venue where motion pictures were shown in the early 1900s. It was not until 1912 that purpose-built cinemas were opened in the area. Later came a demand for larger, more comfortable establishments, which was met by the opening of the Caley in 1923. Then came the talkies in 1927, followed by the opening of more cinemas with some pretentions to comfort—such as the Blue Halls and the Rutland—and, finally, the big super-cinemas such as the Regal, opened in 1938. In the 1950s came the wide screen and stereophonic sound, calling for structural alterations with reductions in the number of seats. The rise in television ownership possibly contributed to the decline in cinema-going. In Tollcross the decrease in population may also have contributed to the closing of smaller cinemas with a purely local audience. Many cinemas were closed, but the Regal (now the Cannon) adapted successfully by converting its one big auditorium to three small ones. There continued to be a demand for classic or special interest films, which is now met by the Filmhouse and by the reopened Cameo.

The theatres too were having problems. The Palladium, converted from a cinema in 1933, was closed and has now been demolished. Audiences were falling, particularly at the Lyceum, which in 1964 was threatened with closure. The outcome, both for the Lyceum and the King's, was to become owned and subsidised by the local authority.

For three weeks each year, since 1947, the Lyceum, King's and Usher Hall become three of the main venues for Edinburgh's International Festival, with many artists of world fame taking part.

Theatre shows, films, concerts—these are what might be called 'spectator' entertainments. Other forms of entertainment, calling for active participation, also flourish. Eating and drinking could come under this heading. Here we have to make an admission: the history of Tollcross pubs deserves a whole chapter in itself, and it is one that we have not researched. All we can say is that licensed premises in the area have long been numerous. As to eating out, the proliferation of national specialities—Italian, Turkish, Chinese and Indian—is an interesting development of recent years.

Other forms of entertainment have included roller skating in Fountainbridge, which enjoyed a vogue in the 1880s and the early 1900s. There was also ice skating on a rink at Lochrin, which was in operation in 1912, but was taken over by a firm of motor dealers in 1920. Ballroom dancing reached the height of its popularity from the 1920s to the 1940s, and continued until the 1960s. Scottish country dancing was also popular, especially in the 1950s. The Palais de Danse in Fountainbridge and the New Cavendish in West Tollcross were the main venues. Later, bingo became the fashion, mainly (though by no means entirely) among older people, while for young people there was a new style of dancing in discotheques.

Snooker and billiards have long been popular, and there were formerly a number of snooker and billiard halls—there was one just beyond the Palais de Danse in Fountainbridge, which in the 1930s was called 'the Trevelyan Billiard Saloon'. Another was above the Tollcross Cinema, where the sign 'Billiards' is still visible high on the building, nearly opposite Glen Street. Today a centre in Grove Street offers snooker as well as other activities. There was also a gambling club in the 1960s, The Grafton, which replaced a restaurant of the same name.

Night clubs are a recent development. Among the more bizarre features of a leisure-centred age is the transformation of the old meat market in Fountainbridge into a night club and restaurant, with a special feature being made of the old meat hook chains hanging from the original steel girders.

Cooke's Circus

Among the individual enterprises, Cooke's Circus was the first major development. It was established first near the site of the Caledonian Hotel in 1835, then moved to Nicolson Street, later the site of the Empire Theatre. In February 1877 John Henry Cooke (son of the founder) opened his equestrian palace in Grindlay Street, where the Lyceum now stands. The programme included several equestrian turns, one by John Henry himself, and one by Ernestine Rosa Cooke, 'the *pet* of the public, Scotland's Première Equestrienne'.

Just six years later the site was taken over for the building of the Lyceum Theatre which opened in September 1883. Cooke then established a new circus in East Fountainbridge which opened on 8 November 1886 with 'the leading Artistes in the Equestrian, Gymnastic and Athletic Professions' including 'Edina Marion Cooke' (sister of Ernestine) 'the infant Horse-Breaker, aged four-and-a-half years, on her pet pony—"Bon Accord".' The cast also included 'highly trained horses and ponies, dogs, pigeons and goats'.

Between 1883 and 1886 Cooke certainly would not have been idle. He also operated circuses in Leith, and he toured Greenock, Perth, Aberdeen, Dundee and Paisley. the entertainment he offered was varied: a 1910 programme included (as well as equestrian turns), 'La Belle Sylvia West, Dainty Vocalist and Dancer', 'Horton and Onda, Chinese Comedians', 'Lily and Elsie Judge and their Wonderful Cockatoos', and many others.

Cooke was not alone in the field. There were show grounds at Gibson Terrace and Ponton Street where carnivals, circuses and menageries were held by other operators such as Bostock and Wombell's.

The Palladium

Picture shows were creeping in. From 1908 onwards, picture shows were held in Cooke's circus, the screen being hung in the centre of the ring so that patrons entering from High Riggs—the cheaper seats—saw it from behind, with the captions in mirror writing. On 11 February 1911 the circus closed down, and was almost immediately reopened as the Palladium picture house. Cooke died in poverty in Edinburgh in 1917.

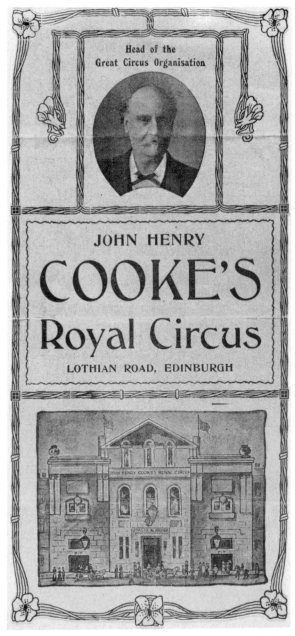

Fig 5.2: The history of Cooke's Circus spans several generations but the most famous member of the family was John Henry Cooke. The portrait is of him in 1910. Cooke's premises in Lothian Road opened in 1835 but were closed by the late 1860s.

The subsequent history of the Palladium is rather strange. Contrary to the usual pattern it changed in 1933 from a cinema to a theatre, and for one year in between—December 1932 to December 1933—it functioned once more as a circus. It advertised as 'Pinder's Palladium Royal Circus Fountainbridge, no connection with the late J H Cooke'. As a theatre it opened with Millicent Ward and her repertory players, but later specialised mainly in variety shows. Eventually it became a night club, and was known as 'Valentino's' before its demolition in 1985.

Poole's (Synod Hall)

The earliest theatre in Tollcross was the West End Theatre in Castle Terrace, opened in 1875. Its exterior, designed by James Gowans, was impressive, no less than was the extravagant style of the neighbouring block of flats which he also designed. The interior too was on a daunting scale, perhaps too daunting for the manager to cope with. At all events the theatre closed in April 1887. The building was sold to the United Presbyterian Church who converted it to a Synod Hall and offices.

In 1902 the premises were acquired by Edinburgh Corporation who let them out for a variety of purposes. These included, over the years, a bowling alley, rifle range, dancing schools, and meetings of the Royal Geographical Society. It is not known exactly when they first rented accommodation in the Hall to Poole's, but it may have been in 1906 when 'the first visit of Charles W Poole's Myriorama' was advertised.

Fig 5.3: The indoor bowling alley at Poole's Synod Hall in 1961. It was thought, when originally opened, to be the first of its kind in Edinburgh.

The Poole family experimented with many unusual lighting and sound effects, the most notable of which was a series of 'Diorama Shows' at Christmas. By the 1920s they were presenting some of the greatest silent films of the day such as *The Four Horsemen of the Apocalypse* and *Covered Wagon*. The Pooles were always great innovators: they introduced children's matinees, and in 1926 they even tried out their own first sound picture, a Scots comedy called *Till the Bells do Ring*. In 1928 the Diorama was shown for the last time and the hall became a permanent cinema venue. As a result they were ready to show the first talkies as early as 1929. In the early 1930s they concentrated on action and adventure films, but after that they began to specialise more and more on horror films. The atmosphere of the building with its maze of dark corridors and seemingly endless doors was particularly suitable for such productions. But the City Council had conceived the grandiose plan of an Opera House. The period of Poole's lease shortened to six months. In desperation Mr Poole put up a notice 'This hall transferred to Edinburgh Ratepayers' and shut up shop in 1966. The site of Poole's is now Edinburgh's well known 'hole in the ground'.

The Lyceum Theatre

By this time the West End Theatre had long been forgotten. The Lyceum, with more modest beginnings, met with continuing success, thanks to effective management by J B Howard and F W P Wyndham. At its opening on 10 September 1883, Henry Irving and Ellen Terry appeared for a fortnight with a series of plays which included Irving's greatest success, *The Bells*. Over the next thirty years Irving continued to appear at the theatre, as did other famous actors and actresses (some of them managing their own companies) such as Frank Benson, Charles Hawtrey, Herbert Beerbohm Tree, Mrs Patrick Campbell, Marie Lohr, Lily Langtry. The Carl Rosa Opera Company appeared more or less regularly, and besides this more serious fare there were many visits from burlesques and popular comics. There was pantomime too, but with the opening of the King's Theatre in 1906 the Lyceum specialised in straight drama and opera.

With the First World War, the era of the great actor-managers was largely ended, although Frank Benson continued into the 1920s. A practice grew up of touring West End successes with secondary companies, but this did not prevent the Lyceum from securing the appearance of many leading actors. Among them were Frank Benson in *Hamlet*, 1926; Fay Compton (sister of Compton Mackenzie, who was also associated with the theatre) in Barrie's *Mary Rose*, 1927; Gladys Cooper in Somerset Maugham's *The Letter*, 1928.

About this time Brandon Thomas was engaged to form a resident company for the theatre. Their greatest success was *Swords about the Cross*, 1936, a play based on the life of Mary Queen of Scots by Margot Lister, who was one of the actresses in the company. The policy of the company was 'no stars', but some actors and actresses were specially popular, notably Joan Kingdon and Wilson Barrett. In 1939 Wilson Barrett—grandson of one of the great nineteenth-century actor-managers—took over a company, which operated under his leadership till 1950. Barrett encouraged Scottish acting talent, putting on plays mainly by well known twentieth-century authors such as Shaw, Barrie, Maugham and Coward.

In 1947 came the International Festival, in which the Lyceum scored several firsts—including the first new play (T S Elliot's *The Cocktail Party*, 1949) and the first late night review to form part of the official programme (*Beyond the Fringe*, 1960). Several French plays were put on—indeed even before the Festival, in 1945, the Comèdie Francaise had appeared for a week at the Lyceum.

Royalty visited the theatre in the 1930s, four times; in 1946, when King George VI and Queen Elizabeth came to Edinburgh for the victory celebrations; in 1962, when a special performance of *Rob Roy* was put on for the state visit of King Olaf of Norway; and in 1977 when a visit was paid by the Queen in her Jubilee Year. The author was present at *Rob Roy* and recalls it vividly: the spirited performance, the programmes printed on silk, the auditorium decorated lavishly with red carnations and, in the audience, the flash of family tiaras vainly attempting to emulate the Queen's. What fun to be present, once in a lifetime, at such a brilliant occasion. But no less fun to recall many other first class theatrical experiences at the Lyceum. Perhaps *The Life of Galileo*, *The Crucible* and *The Prime of Miss Jean Brodie* stand out the most.

During the late 1950s the Lyceum fell on hard times. Except for the three weeks of the Festival, and the Christmas period when the Fol de Rols appeared, audiences were small. In fact the theatre was no longer viable. In 1961 it was purchased by Mr Meyer Oppenheim who had plans for developing the whole site, including that of the Synod Hall. Thus began the great saga of Edinburgh's 'hole in the ground'. So far as the Lyceum is concerned, the outcome was that in 1964, just as it was about to close, the City of Edinburgh bought it from Mr Oppenheim and set up a Trust to operate it.

Since then there have been changes of direction, but the Lyceum's high standards have remained unchanged. In 1977 its interior was renovated. The author, being a regular attender, can testify to many good performances in the past two or three years including Shakespeare, Wilde, Noel Coward, and Molière in Scots.

The Albert Hall

After the Royal Lyceum, the next place of entertainment to be opened in (or rather on the edge of) our area was the Albert Hall in Shandwick Place, which on 7 April 1884 advertised 'Poole's Mammoth Diorama' supported by a company of star artistes. Various other entertainments were advertised over the years, for example a mesmerist in 1887, and mission meetings were also held there. On 28 September 1908 moving pictures were introduced: they were advertised as 'B and B (Bright and Beautiful)', possibly indicating a superior moral as well as visual quality. From about 1915 it was known as the West End Cinema. It could not, however, stand up to the competition of newer cinemas and it closed some time in the early 1930s. The building became a cafe, but is now private accommodation.

Next came the Palladium, in 1886. We have already outlined its career, first as a circus, then as a cinema, then a theatre, and finally a night club until it was demolished.

The New Pavilion Theatre

On 15 February 1897 the New Pavilion Theatre—later the Pavilion Theatre, known as the Piv—opened in Grove Street. Moving pictures were being shown there in 1902. It became in succession the Prince of Wales Theatre of Varieties (March 1906) the Alhambra Theatre of Varieties, under new management (September 1906) and Pringle's Picture Palace (1908). Finally in December 1917 it reopened as the Garrick Theatre, presenting a revue with a wartime theme, *Hullo Baby*. It was destroyed by fire in June 1921. Today, Grove Street has once more an entertainment facility: a leisure centre with snooker, squash and a children's indoor fun centre.

The King's Theatre

The King's Theatre opened on 8 December 1906, with *Cinderella* with Zena Dare in the name part and Violet Englefield as Principal Boy. One scene was a beautiful spring glade with real rabbits grazing on the slope. This might not be to today's taste, but it strikes the note of way-out extravagance which makes the King's Theatre pantomimes such a joy today.

At this time Edinburgh's three main theatres—the King's, Royal Lyceum and Theatre Royal—were all under the management of Howard and Wyndham, and it became the policy for the King's to specialise in pantomime and lavish musicals, the Lyceum in straight drama and the Theatre Royal in music hall. But there were plays too at the King's, including in 1912 a racing drama *The Whip* with an express train in one scene and four race horses pelting along on treadmills in another. In 1916 Sarah Bernhardt appeared— no doubt in a less rackety performance. Since then many great actors and actresses have appeared at the King's in straight plays, including Sir John Martin Harvey, Noel Coward, Gertrude Lawrence, Fay Compton, Ingrid Bergman, John Gielgud (in *Hamlet*) and Lawrence Olivier (in *The Entertainer* and *Othello*). But perhaps the names that one associates most readily with the King's are those of the comedy stars such as Harry Lauder, Stanley Lupino, Nellie Wallace—later Will Fyfe, Dave Willis, Harry Gordon—and their successors today, Jimmy Logan, Stanley Baxter, Rikki Fulton and others. For some years the *Five Past* and *Half Past Eight* shows were regular features.

Scottish Opera and Scottish Ballet make regular appearances at the King's, and during the Festival there have been many outstanding performances by foreign opera and ballet companies.

From 1922 onwards the theatre has been used for several weeks each year by amateur companies, such as the Southern Light Opera, the Bohemians and the Gang Show. These are of a high standard and always attract large audiences.

In general, as with the Lyceum, audiences were dwindling in the 1950s and 1960s; and in the late 1960s the King's was taken over by the City of Edinburgh. In 1985 the theatre was refurbished, with new seating, new curtains and a spacious orchestra pit. This soon paid off in increased audiences. Since then there have been some notable performances, including straight plays, opera, ballet, and pantomime. The local authorities deserve our gratitude for keeping these two theatres open.

The Palais de Danse

From the opening of the King's in 1906 we move on to 1911, when purpose-built cinemas began to proliferate. Perhaps the Coliseum at 125 Fountainbridge, opened in 1911, can scarcely be so described, since it was 'a transformation effected on the interior of the one-time Grand Roller Skating Rink'. With accommodation for 1500, the Coliseum was the largest picture house in the city. In 1920 the Palais de Danse, with the same address as the Coliseum, was opened by the Palais de Danse and Cinema Company; and the two enterprises ran jointly until the cinema closed in December 1942. The Palais de Danse continued to flourish. The great era of ballroom dancing, at its prime from the 1920s to the 1940s, was not yet over. There were refinements such as a balcony in which one could take tea while watching the dancing, and a revolving stage with two bands which took over from one another to provide continuous music. A photograph from the 1950s shows an elegant line-up of couples taking part in the regional heat of a dance contest. Then, as time went on, less formal styles began to appear: Victor Sylvester's quick-quick-slow was giving place to jiving, and then to rock. Here is a recent letter in the *Evening News*:

> 'I learned to jive at the Fountainbridge Palais early in 1958. For one shilling (5p) you could dance on a Tuesday evening to records. The records I learned to jive to were "Let's go to the hop" by Danny and the Juniors, "Gotta lotta livin to do" and "Jailhouse Rock". . . The manager was an ex all-in wrestler called Bruno. He was a big, pleasant guy, but he and his army of bouncers ruthlessly ejected any would-be hard men who tried to interrupt the dancing.'

By 1967 the fashion for ballroom dancing was on the wane and bingo was becoming popular. The owners of the hall, Mecca, renamed it 'The Palais' and reopened it as a bingo club. In this capacity it still flourishes; indeed it is said to be catering for a larger, and younger, membership over recent years.

The Early Cinemas

Tollcross Cinema, variously named as the New Tollcross or more simply as Toll X, opened at 140 Lauriston Place on Hogmanay 1912. In its early history

Fig 5.4: A theatrical ball held in the Palais de Danse, Fountainbridge, in 1932. Mr Poole, who owned cinemas in Edinburgh, can be seen standing on the extreme left hand side of the group.

it tried to set itself above its rivals by having reservable seats and by advertising that it was 'the Distinctively Different Theatre'. Due to lack of patronage it was forced to close in 1942–3 and became a furniture store.

On 8 January 1914 the King's Cinema opened at 38 Home Street. In 1949 it came under the management of the Poole family and reopened as the Cameo, specialising in continental films, its small size being appropriate for the audiences which these films attracted. The Cameo opened with Michelle Morgan in *La Symphonie Pastorale*. Russian classics too, such as *Peter the Great* and *The Battleship Potemkin* were shown. It was the first cinema in Edinburgh to have a milk bar, and the first to obtain a drink licence. It closed in 1982, but has been reopened under new management in 1987, once again presenting predominantly *avant garde* films.

The Usher Hall

The year 1914 saw another important opening: that of the Usher Hall, built with the aid of a bequest of £100 000 made in 1896 by Andrew Usher the brewer. The choice of a site had presented much difficulty—Atholl Crescent was one suggested location. The final choice involved the demolition of Lothian Road Public School, to be replaced by Tollcross School which was built on the site of the old slaughterhouse in Fountainbridge. The design of the hall, by an English architect, J Stockdale Harrison, who won the open competition, is described in *Buildings of Scotland* as 'a notable Beaux-Arts performance executed with the utmost suavity and precision'. Its exterior is adorned with statuary by several different sculptors representing 'Municipal Beneficence', 'The Soul of Music', and other appropriate themes. The Edwardian high quality of the interior is exhibited in the mahogany fitments of the cloakrooms and in the panels of Sienna marble that line the staircases.

At the opening concert Eleanore Osborne sang from Tannhauser 'Charmed Hall of Song, I give thee greeting . . . how proud, how grand dost thou appear!' Today the Usher Hall is criticised on various grounds, such as the acoustics, the deficiencies of the organ and the lack of refreshment facilities; yet these opening words still do not seem out of place. How astounded would Eleanore Osborne's (no doubt highly select) audience have been, had they known that seventy-three years later (9 August 1987) a concert from the hall was to be broadcast live to an audience of 600 million viewers in the Soviet Union, the Eastern bloc and in Western Europe!

In keeping with the terms of Usher's bequest, the hall is let mainly for concerts, catering for a wide range of tastes: pipe bands, military bands, jazz, folk, gospel singers, classical symphony and chamber concerts. For large choirs, such as the Edinburgh Royal Choral Union, it is a particularly suitable venue, and the Choral Union's annual performance of *The Messiah* on New Year's Day has become an Edinburgh tradition. So too have the weekly concerts of the Scottish National Orchestra on Fridays in winter, for which season tickets may be obtained. The opening concert of the Festival is regularly held in the hall and is widely broadcast, though never before so widely as

Fig 5.5: Even the surrounding houses were involved in the celebrations to mark the laying of the foundation stone of the Usher Hall in 1911.

mentioned above. Among the many distinguished artistes who have performed there, none was more loved than Kathleen Ferrier, the contralto singer, who last appeared there in September 1952, a year before her untimely death. She is commemorated by a bronze bust in the assembly area.

Meetings and lectures which are thought likely to attract large audiences are also held here. In the winter 1974–5 there was even a proposal to book the hall for a circus, with *The Scotsman* delicately explaining that 'any debris they (the performing animals) leave in the hall will be swept aside to allow the Scottish National Orchestra to give concerts'. Fortunately this proposal was not adopted. In all its varied uses, the Usher Hall may be said to have been a continuing success and is one of Edinburgh's major assets.

Maxime's (later New Cavendish) Ballroom

Our list of dates now shows a big gap, as the First World War intervenes. During the war cinemas and theatres continued to provide much needed entertainment, but there were no new openings. After the war came the boom in ballroom dancing. As already mentioned, the Coliseum Cinema added a dance hall to its establishment, and about the same time—in the 1920s—Maxime's ballroom was opened in West Fountainbridge, in premises formerly occupied by a riding school. One of its rooms, used for dancing and functions, was called 'the Wellington Room'—perhaps an echo of this equestrian connection. During the 1930s there was some trouble relating to law and order—we have not inquired into the details—and the hall was closed. It remained closed, except for a short period when a tenant ran it as 'The Cavendish', until Christmas 1940. It was then reopened by Tim Wright as 'The New Cavendish'. Throughout the war it was very popular, and in particular was much patronised by the Polish troops stationed locally. After the war it continued to flourish. There were regular Old Time and Scottish Country Dancing sessions. After Tim Wright's death in 1960 it was carried on by Andrew Bathgate until 1972, when it was acquired by new owners who ran it under the name of 'Clouds'. Today as 'Coasters' it still provides a venue for dancing.

The Later Cinemas

With the end of the war we come into the age of the big cinemas, with greater pretensions to comfort; and of these the first to appear in Tollcross was the Caley, which opened on 1 January 1923. It had seating for 900. In December 1929 after the reconstruction, which increased the seating to 2100, it reopened for talkies.

In the 1950s the Caley was the first cinema in Edinburgh to combine the wide-screen cinema-scope with stereophonic sound. This entailed a reduction in seating to 1800. In this new medium the Caley presented *The Robe* and *The Prime of Miss Jean Brodie*. It was earlier associated with the Edinburgh

Film Guild for whom it presented special Sunday shows, and also with the Edinburgh Film Festival. By 1984 it had ceased to present films alone, but was also being used for musical shows. From 1984 it was partially open for cabaret; it then closed for a time, and reopened as the Amphitheatre night club in the autumn of 1986.

Catering for a more local audience, the Blue Halls, Lauriston Street, opened on 1 January 1930. *White Cargo* was the film presented. Its Saturday matinees were extremely popular with the children of Tollcross as only one penny admission was charged, and sometimes a jam jar was accepted instead of currency. In 1954 it closed with *Tarzan Triumphs*, to reopen, renamed the Beverley, with *The Robe*—for which cinemascope and stereophonic sound had been installed. Due to falling audiences it closed down in 1959, the last shows being *Carousel* and *Yacht on the High Seas*. On 24 April 1930 the Rutland Picture House, one of the first of the super cinemas, opened in Canning Street. This must have been an impressive opening, featuring as it did Lyndon Laird at the Mighty Organ and Norman Austin with the Rutland Symphony Orchestra. In 1950 the cinema was taken over by new owners and renamed the Gaumont. Its last show on 30 May 1963 was *Taxi for Tobruk*. That night a fire broke out, damaging the cinema so severely that it was later demolished.

On 10 October 1938 an even larger and more luxurious cinema, the Regal, opened in Lothian Road with *Vessels of Wrath*, featuring Charles Laughton and Elsa Lanchester. It was also known as the ABC (Associated British Cinemas). Built on the site of the former Port Hopetoun Canal Basin, it had seating for nearly 3000, with comforts such as air conditioning and generous space between the seats, and a cafe adjoining. In 1955 it acquired stereophonic sound, and until the late 1950s it was able to attract large audiences from all over Edinburgh. Television, however, was becoming increasingly popular, with devastating effects on cinema attendances. The management adapted to this situation by deciding to create three smaller cinemas out of the big one. On 29 November 1964 the then Secretary of State for Scotland, William Ross, performed the opening ceremony of the new triple cinema, showing a triple bill of *Goodbye Mr Chips*, *Ice Station Zebra*, and *Moon Zero Two*. In that form the Regal—now known as the Cannon—has flourished to this day.

In 1975 the old Lothian Road Church was bought by Filmhouse Limited. This company was established by the Film Guild. Its two cinemas are now the main venues of the International Film Festival every August; during the rest of the year the Filmhouse provides an excellent restaurant, and wine bar, and presents a programme of outstanding international classics.

Conclusion

So in spite of the inroads of television it can be said that, with *avant garde* films showing at the Cameo, international classics at Filmhouse, and with good audiences for more general interest films at the Cannon, the cinema is alive and well and living in Tollcross. So too is the theatre, though with the help of subsidies from the District Council. Concerts, both classical and popular, attract large audiences, and their coverage has been greatly widened through radio and television. Other forms of entertainment also flourish. Discos have replaced the old dance halls, multi-purpose games centres have come in place of the snooker and billiard halls, and night clubs have entered the scene.

Thus Tollcross is still an entertainment centre. In fact it could claim to be Edinburgh's foremost entertainment centre. Crowds pour into it at Festival time. Leven Street becomes impassable as the audience surges out from the pantomime or from seeing their talented friends perform in the latest amateur show. On Friday and Saturday nights the streets are thronged with people making their choice of a national specialty restaurant, going off to dance, or just going for a drink. There are queues for the cinema.

All this brings problems. In particular, the number of licensed premises in Tollcross has given some concern to local residents because of its effect on the character of the area. A 1986 survey by the Community Council found that in a square mile of the Tollcross area there were thirty public houses, twenty-six licensed restaurants, and ten licensed theatres, cinemas and discos. All these in an area of dwindling population. So one thing is clear: Tollcross, perhaps sometimes to its own discomfort, is providing an entertainment and leisure service far beyond its own boundaries.

Further reading

1 Baird, George, (1963). *Edinburgh Theatres, Cinemas and Circuses 1820–1963*. Type-script, Edinburgh Room, Central Public Library, Edinburgh.
2 Campbell, Donald, (1983). *A Brighter Sunshine: A Hundred Years of the Royal Lyceum Theatre*.
3 Thomas, Brendan, (1984). *The Last Picture Shows*.

6

Schooling

Catherine Toall

Introduction

In the relatively small area of our study there have been over twenty educational establishments of remarkably differing character and historical background. Although it is not within the scope of this chapter to explain the history of education and relate it to these establishments, much of the information offered will give the reader some opportunity to get the general flavour of changes in education over the last three centuries.

For the most part this chapter describes and illustrates schools in the area, but this is not the full story. Few would know that, last century, there were two Riding Academies in the area and a Military and Naval Academy. We have also included information on the College of Art and of evening classes for adults at the turn of the century. There was also a day release and evening Commercial Institute which was a forerunner of modern further education colleges.

Before State Education at an elementary level was introduced in 1872, there were many Church aided and secular schools in the area, such as Castlebarns Industrial School, the Vennel Ragged Feeding School and Lothian Road Church School, dealing mainly with the huge population of uneducated children, more often than not from poor and destitute families.

Larger scale attempts to provide an education for the sons and daughters of unfortunate merchants include some of Edinburgh's most prestigious schools which had an early history in the area, some of which are still to be found here: George Heriot's, George Watson's, Mary Erskine's and James Gillespie's.

As State education provision grew there were a large number of primary schools in the area. Even in such a small street as Glen Street there were two schools: St Ignatius Roman Catholic School and All Saints Episcopal School facing one another. Darroch Secondary School, originally Gilmore Primary School, followed the inception of Boroughmuir and St Thomas of Aquins School and, by 1930 the first Edinburgh Corporation Nursery School was opened in West Tollcross.

Each educational establishment (numbered in the text) can be located on the map within this Chapter.

Fig 6.1: The qualifying class from All Saints' School in 1926. The School is in the background.

Schools

All Saints' Episcopal School (1)
One of two schools in Glen Street, this Episcopal School was built behind the Church of All Saints in 1878. The Church had been built in 1867 and the school had originally been established a year later at 91 West Port.

The school was financed from 'School Pence', voluntary contributions, Church collections, and Sales held in the school. The weekly 'School Pence' rate was twopence, and one penny for infants, which helped towards the education of the children and to pay the teachers' salaries which, by the middle of last century was £52 and £14 for the assistants, per annum.

By the 1950s it had become obvious that the school was not serving the Episcopalian population. In 1957 a report by the Director of Education showed that only eleven per cent of the pupils had Episcopalian parents and in 1958, after agreement by representatives from the Episcopal Church in Scotland, the School closed for good. The building, however, still stands in Glen Street to this day and is owned by a firm of Architects.

Boroughmuir (2)
Before the Education Act of 1900, higher education was only available at the merchant Company Schools, George Heriot's, or the Royal High School. After 1900 as demand for such free advanced education increased the Education Committee decided to build two secondary schools, Boroughmuir and Brough-ton.

Boroughmuir was originally to have been called Victorian Higher Grade School but the Secretary of State felt he could not recommend the name to King Edward. Because of its position on the ancient Burgh Muir it was so named. Built in 1904 on the corner of Warrender Park Terrace and White-house Loan it is now occupied by Boroughmuir Junior School.

The demand for admission was so great that soon the need for a larger school was felt. By 1914 the present building was erected (the Links School was taken over by James Gillespie's in 1922) and was officially opened by the Secretary of State J McKinnon Wood who, while making his speech, had a large bag of flour thrown at him by a suffragette!

Having a large Dining Hall, the school offered lunches at very reasonable prices. In 1927 you could buy soup for one penny, a meat course for five pence and pudding for a penny halfpenny. However, a set three course meal would work out cheaper at sixpence halfpenny. At that time the Headmaster would have earned only £500 a year and Masters only half that amount. Women teachers of French and English would have earned only £150 a year and Janitors a measly one pound seven shillings and sixpence a week!

The School boasts many clubs and societies. There are so many available that there must be something to suit all tastes. For the more adventurous is the Cairngorm Mountaineering Club, founded by the Headmaster in 1947.

The school badge depicts the raising of the Scottish Standard, reputedly by Bonnie Prince Charlie, over the Bore Stone, as he approached Edinburgh, in the eighteenth century.

Castlebarns Industrial School (3)
In 1843 the first Industrial School was opened in Aberdeen. A better title might have been 'industrious' as the school was merely providing an elementary education with one or two meals a day for 'a class of poor children, the outcasts of society, either from the neglect or carelessness of unthinking parents, or from their immoral or dissipated habits.'

In 1849 St Cuthbert's Church Session bought a house with garden and park at Castlebarns (now Morrison Street) and established its Industrial School. It was situated between Gardner's Crescent and Semple Street beside St Cuthbert's Bakery, in premises also known as St Cuthbert's mission.

The School was financed initially by the congregation but in 1885 the Kirk Session placed the school under the Scottish Education Department. By 1902 numbers had dwindled and it was closed down. The premises continued to be used for congregational activities until 1967 when, given the heavy expenditure necessary to renovate the building, it was demolished.

The College of Art (4)
The College of Art began in 1907 after a merger between the School of the Board of Manufacturers, the Royal Scottish Academy Life School, the School of Applied Art and the Art Department of Heriot-Watt College. In July 1907 the Prince of Wales (to become George V) laid the foundation stone of the new building on the site of the former Cattlemarket, and, in January 1909, the College moved into its new home.

By the 1960s the College had grown to accommodate 800 students and the need for expansion was realised by the purchase of property in the neighbourhood. In 1974 it was then possible to build a major extension to the College at a cost of £1.5 million from the Scottish Education Department. Called the Hunter Building after a former College Principal, it was officially opened by Lord Robbins, former Chairman of the Coal Board, in June 1977.

Among its many achievements, at the request of a Japanese Trade Delegation to Scotland in 1968, paintings, glass ornaments and jewellery, made by students at the College, were shipped to Tokyo for a special exhibition. In 1986 staff and students made a magnificent stained glass window for the Royal Scots Garrison Church in Werl, West Germany.

Darroch School (5)
Darroch School was built in 1908 but was originally called Gilmore Place Primary School. However, in 1928 the Education Committee decided to convert the school into a three year secondary school to be named after the late chairman of the committee, Professor Darroch.

The pupils, known as Darrochians, were placed into four inter-school houses, Gilmore (green), Home (red), Leven (yellow) and Melville (blue). The School badge, shaped as a shield, had an oak-leaf in the centre, being a symbol of strength and loyalty.

As with most schools, sport played a part in the curriculum. Football was the main sport for years and many games were even arranged between masters and boys. In later years rugby became popular.

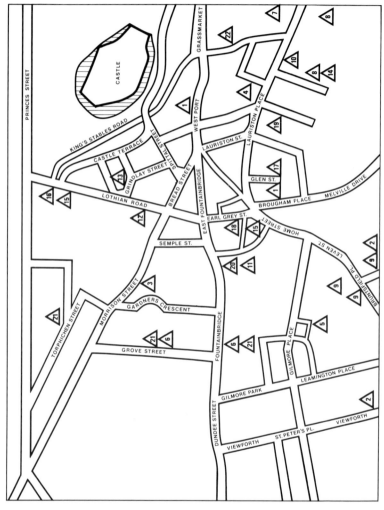

Fig 6.2: Map of the area showing where the schools and college were and are located.

A large five roomed flat at 5 Leamington Terrace was purchased in 1939 and was known as the 'School Flat'. It was used by girls on the Domestic course who were learning housewifery.

In the early 1960s Darroch was chosen by the Scottish Education Department to launch an experimental course in Modern Studies which is a subject still taught today.

Pupils with the necessary qualifications could go on to Boroughmuir School to study for Highers and, in August 1962, Darroch sent its biggest intake there. This was at a time when the school roll had been increasing steadily and at one stage an annexe at Bruntsfield Primary School had to be brought into use.

Such overcrowding, however, was one of the complaints against the school in 1968 when an Edinburgh solicitor initiated a public outcry against the school, described as a slum and fit only for demolition. 'Decent parents,' he said, 'are being forced out of the State system' and that, instead of proposing huge expenditure on the building of an Opera House at Castle Terrace, more money should be spent on rebuilding schools.

Although Darroch ceased to be a Junior Secondary School in the 1970s it has since functioned as an annexe for both James Gillespie and Boroughmuir schools.

Fountainbridge Public School (6)
Fountainbridge Public School started out its life in 61 Grove Street before moving into a purpose-built school at 88 Fountainbridge in 1874, nearly opposite the top of Grove Street at Fountain Court. It was to accommodate 750 children, but to do this, yet leave enough space for a playground, meant that the building had to be of a height greater than was deemed desirable.

Because it was built beside the busy road of Fountainbridge the classrooms were built in such a way that they were set back from the road, forming an open courtyard between the two connecting wings.

On the ground floor was the Infant School and the older age group were taught in the rooms above. The upper classroom was 28ft high, measured to the open timbered roof, and heating was provided by two open fires.

By 1918 there had been many changes in the schooling needs in the area and new Schools had been built (Gilmore Place, Bruntsfield and Tollcross). Although Fountainbridge School closed for the teaching of children in that year, it was taken over by the Commercial Institute which had previously used the Grove Street accommodation and which later moved to Torphichen Street School in 1932.

For a decade Fountainbridge School became a Schools' kitchen and dinners were sent out to many schools in hay-boxes to keep them warm. The classrooms above were used as a voluntary recreation and hobbies club for the unemployed and, at the beginning of the war, they were taken over by the Western Athletic Club.

In 1941 the kitchen and classrooms were used for the first British Restaurant, the 'Naebours Tryst' which provided cheap and nourishing food at a time when rationing was in force during the war.

From 1954 to its closure in 1963 the School was described as Edinburgh School of Building (West Fountainbridge Annexe) where, among other things it catered for day release brickwork classes for handicapped boys, maths and drawing classes, and evening classes.

George Heriot's School (7)

When he died in 1624, Geroge Heriot, a wealthy goldsmith, left in his will the sum of £23 625.10s 3½d for the purposes of building a residential school (originally called a Hospital) for boys whose (Merchant) parents had died or suffered great misfortune.

A site was chosen on the lands of High Riggs called Heriot's Wark and the Royal Master Mason, William Wallace, was commisioned to design the building, although he died in 1631 before his work was finished. William Ayton, his assistant and successor, whose portrait still hangs in the school, carried on his work until 1650 when the building was eventually completed, twenty-two years after the first foundation stone was laid.

The major reason for the long delay in completing the building work was caused by slow collection of debts owed to George Heriot, mainly by the Crown. However, the outbreak of the Civil War brought more difficulties and, in 1650, before its original function could be realised, Cromwell's Scottish Military Government took forcible possession and turned it into a military hospital. It was not until 1659 that the building was restored to the Governors and, in April of that year, thirty boys were admitted.

For over three hundred years George Heriot's has remained one of Edinburgh's foremost educational establishments, whose history during this period is beyond the scope of this work. As a final word though, George Heriot's admitted girls to the school for the first time in September 1979.

George Watson's College (8)

George Watson's College, now situated at Colinton Road, started out its life in a seven acre field owned by George Heriot's Trustees in Lauriston, built between 1738 and 1741, and was first known as Watson's Merchant Academy.

Its founder came from a family of well known Edinburgh Merchants and, on his death in 1723, he left £144 000 Scots pounds for the purpose of building a residential school, or hospital, for the support and education of boys whose parents or grandparents had been Merchants, but who through death or other misfortune were not able to provide for them.

In June 1741 ninety Foundationers (supported pupils) were admitted to the new School. The Foundationers were dressed in a uniform of dark green corduroy, round black caps with black glazed shades. Many hundreds of these pupils had passed through the school by 1870, when the governors applied to become a day school, after the Endowed Institution Act was passed that year which abolished the Hospital system of education.

Larger premises were required to house the new day school. The proposed rebuilding of the Royal Infirmary also required land upon which Watson's was built. However, adjacent to Watson's in Archibald Place was the Merchant

Maidens' Hospital which, in 1870, decided to set up a day school in Queen Street. Because both schools belonged to the Merchant Company of Edinburgh, Watson's was easily able to move into the vacated premises. Soon after they extended the building to include a new gymnasium, science and physics laboratories and an elementary department.

The old building was incorporated into the Royal Infirmary and, when the foundation stone of the Infirmary was laid, a choir of a hundred Watson's boys were selected to lead the Hymns. Again, in the 1930s, the Infirmary planned an expansion, and Watson's purchased a site in the Merchiston Castle estate where a purpose built school was erected and opened in 1932.

To celebrate the move and to bid farewell to the old school, Watson's 'old boys' gathered in 1932 from all over Britain, Ireland, the Dominions and the colonies in the true spirit of the College motto—*Ex Corde Caritas*—meaning Love from the Heart.

James Gillespie's School (9)

James Gillespie was a very successful businessman in the snuff trade in the eighteenth century who established a snuff mill in Colinton. He died in 1797 and left most of his fortune for the erection of a Hospital for aged men and women and a School for poor boys.

The Hospital, built in 1802, was situated on the site of the mansion of Wrichtis Housis adjacent to modern day Gillespie Crescent and the School, built in 1803, was within its grounds by Bruntsfield place, facing the Links. Both Institutions were managed by the Edinburgh Merchant Company.

Otherwise known as 'Bruntsfield Links Schule' it took in sixty-five pupils in the first year, teaching for six hours daily in the summer and five hours in the winter. The boys were split into two divisions with one master teaching each.

In 1870, following the Endowed Institution Act, the 'Gillespie Pensioners' had to give up their accommodation in the Hospital which, after a great deal of internal renovation, was turned into a fee-paying school, for girls as well as boys, to replace the Links School. The Board of Governors also awarded bursaries to enable poor children of ability to attend.

In 1908 the Merchant Company was unable to run the school due to financial constraints and the building was taken over by the Edinburgh School Board to become James Gillespie's Primary and Higher Grade School.

When Boroughmuir School vacated the building at the corner of Warrender Park Crescent and Whitehouse Loan in 1914, Gillespie's School moved in, leaving the old Hospital to be sold in 1922 to the Royal Blind Asylum. By 1923, because of overcrowding, the junior school was moved to Warrender Park School in Marchmont Crescent. By 1929 there was a growing demand for a high school for girls so the School Board changed the Marchmont Crescent Junior School into a primary school for boys and created in Warrender Park Terrace the famous James Gillespie's High School for Girls.

In 1966 a new school was built in the grounds of Bruntsfield House with its front gates on to Lauderdale Street, next to the Primary School which is a collection of very inadequate buildings erected earlier in the century.

A decision was made in 1973 to close the Boys' School and to change the Girls' School into a coeducational establishment.

Lauriston Special Public School (10)

This school was set up on 22 January 1912 to accommodate the educational needs of children who suffered from skin diseases. It was situated at 41 Lauriston Place in a specially converted dwelling house, and remained there until the buildings were demolished to make way for an expansion of the Royal Infirmary in the 1970s.

When it was opened thirty-three children were admitted. Of these eighteen were suffering from ringworm and fifteen from scabies. When the children were cured they received a clearing line and sent back to ordinary schools. Unfortunately the School Log book finishes in 1938 and it is not known if it continued for this or a related function between then and 1972 when the building was closed up.

Lochrin Nursery (11)

Before Lochrin Nursery opened its doors for the first time in 1930 there had been a nursery above the Public Wash house, built earlier in the century. An attendant was employed to look after the children while the mothers got on with the washing.

Because of the large demand for such provision and the limited space available above the wash house, the Edinburgh Corporation decided to build its first nursery school on the grounds of Tollcross Public School, immediately facing the wash house.

When the new building opened it catered for forty deprived children from the overcrowded Tollcross and Fountainbridge area. Many of the children were in poor health and would have benefited greatly from the regular meals, the fresh air, the pleasant surroundings and the many toys and activities.

The nursery teacher would have been helped by volunteers to provide an interesting education, including talks on nature, dancing, singing and games. The mothers too were encouraged to learn more about their children's health and education and a mothers' club was formed, one of the main activities being the making of clothes.

In 1939 the Public Health Department took over the nursery and turned it into a clearing station for casualties in the event of an air raid. However, in 1941, it was reopened as a nursery.

Over the next decade many families had moved from the area and widescale demolition of houses had taken place. Because of this the Nursery found itself dealing less with the very poor and undereducated. Changes in staffing also helped to improve the service offered after the introduction of training schemes and qualifications necessary to do the job.

Today the Nursery has places for sixty children, forty part-time and twenty full-time.

Lothian Road Church School (12)

Very little is known about this day school which was set up by Lothian Road

Church in 1845. It was built behind the Church on a site called the 'Chucky Pend' and prospered there until 1859.

A correspondent to the *Evening News* earlier this century remembers playing in the Chucky Pend which we believe got its name from the fact that the ground was covered with small pebbles or chucky stones and probably used by children in their games.

Inside the 'close' were the doors which led to Lothian Road Church Halls, where she attended the Band of Hope and enjoyed magic lantern shows and talent competitions.

Lothian Road School (13)

Lothian Road School was built in 1881 on the corner of Cambridge Street (the School's address) and Grindlay Street, at a cost of £10 791.5s 5d, which included purchase of the site, building and furnishing, and the janitor's house.

Paid for by loans and the city rates, the school came under the auspices of the Edinburgh School Board, and was one of the few which was 'honoured'

Fig 6.3: A street artist at work around 1903. The building in the background is Lothian Road School, demolished later to make way for the Usher Hall.

to be inspected by visitors from the School Board on a regular basis. One of the more notable visitors was Flora Stevenson, after whom a school in Comely Bank was named.

Evening classes for adults were a notable feature of the School, in response (in part) to the self-improvement movement, at the turn of the century. In his journal of 1900 to 1906, a local man, William Anderson, who worked as a coalman with St Cuthbert's Cooperative, describes his good experiences of Lothian Road School classes, although he admits to falling asleep in one of them! Many subjects were available: book-keeping, economics, arithmetic, English, mechanical and engineering drawing, to name but a few.

Apart from evening classes, on a Saturday there were drawing classes for Pupil Teachers, leading towards the Elementary Drawing Certificate of Art and Science. Pupils learned various forms: geometrical, model, light and shade, and freehand.

In 1912 the School closed and the pupils were transferred to the new Tollcross Public School in Fountainbridge, built on the site of the Municipal Slaughterhouse, and now called Tollcross Primary School. Lothian Road School was demolished and on its site the Usher Hall was built in 1914.

Merchant Maidens' Hospital (14)
In 1694 the Merchant Maidens' Hospital was founded by Mary Erskine in the Bristo Port to cater for the daughters of Edinburgh Merchants, in the same way that George Heriot's supported and educated their sons. For over a

Fig 6.4: The Merchant Maidens' Hospital in Lauriston Lane. The hospital remained there from 1818 to 1870.

hundred years it functioned in relatively unsuitable premises, until in 1818 it moved to a purpose built Hospital in Archibald Place, financed by the Merchant Company of Edinburgh.

Although Mary Erskine was an outspoken pioneer in the education of girls, it was not until the late nineteenth century that reading and writing became an important part of the curriculum. Until then the main emphasis was on domestic 'arts' such as spinning lace, dressing meat and household thrift. The girls also had to make their own clothes which, in the early days were made of 'Orkney material' which could be dyed any colour. In the early nineteenth century the uniform was always green.

Apart from making clothes for themselves they also sold shirts for captured French soldiers in the late eighteenth century and in 1785 the Maidens supplied the material for a hot air balloon used by Lunardi. A variety of other work was carried out and the profits accrued were divided among the girls on leaving the Hospital. In 1791 the sum paid to each was £3.6s 8d.

The Hospital's progress was overseen by two of its Governors every week but its day to day business was carried out by the Governess. To become a Governess one had to be 'under thirty years of age, decent, chaste and be able in domestic as well as accounting skills.' She would be as concerned about the morals as well as the education of the girls and be responsible for the behaviour of the School Mistresses, their assistants and servants.

In 1870, when the Hospital system of Education was abolished, the Merchant Maidens' became a day school and moved to the Hopetoun Rooms at the West End of Queen Street, where it became known as Mary Erskine's School for Girls.

Mary Erskine's School is now in Ravelston.

The Royal Academy for Teaching Exercises (15)

More commonly known as the Royal Menage, the Academy was a school of horsemanship, latterly situated in Lothian Road next to the Scottish Naval and Military Academy at the beginning of the nineteenth century.

The Academy was originally founded in 1763 at a time when horsemanship was greatly neglected and it was patronised by many well known citizens of Edinburgh, such as the portrait painter Allan Ramsay. It was situated in Nicolson Street and remained there until 1829 when the Royal College of Surgeons was built.

It moved to Lothian Road and remained there until about 1870 when the Caledonian Railway Company took over the site for their second Edinburgh Station at the west end of Princes Street.

An advertisement appearing in *The Scotsman* in 1845 states:

ROYAL ACADEMY FOR RIDING
Lothian Road

Mr Isaac Scott respectfully intimates that classes for Ladies and Gentlemen are now going on.

The School is comfortably warmed and is very handsomely set up.

Ladies and Gentlemen are invited to visit it and, by their own observations, satisfy themselves of the fact, that as a public establishment, it is not surpassed, if equalled in the Kingdom.

HORSES BROKE IN
Brae House, Edinburgh
January, 1845.

In the 1870s a new Royal Riding Academy appeared at West Tollcross, the former name for the west side of Home Street. This Academy was owned by John Player, at least until the turn of the century, but by 1914 is known to have been owned by a James Fairbairn Player MRCVS. Above his house was a lifesize model of a horse which remained there well into the twentieth century. The Academy itself was converted into the Cavendish Ballroom, and is now used as a Disco complex called 'Coasters'. John Player's house was converted into the Grafton Restaurant and is now occupied by Tokyo Joe's Disco pub.

The Scottish Naval and Military Academy (16)
This little known Academy was situated at the foot of Lothian Road and was built sometime at the beginning of the nineteenth century, probably around 1830. It was owned by the Crown and its main function was to train young men for duty in the Royal and East India Company services, covering such subjects as gun drill, military exercises and military drawing. For a long time it was under the supervision of a former Black Watch officer, Captain John Ord. In 1846 the property is known to have been owned by Isaac Scott who lived in the nearby Kirk Brae House.

The Academy was demolished by 1870 to make way for the Caledonian Railway Company's station in Edinburgh at the west end of Princes Street.

St Ignatius Primary (RC) School (17)
Erected in Glen Street in 1864 (and opposite All Saints' School built in 1878), the school was described a hundred years later as one of the worst in Edinburgh. It had no playground and the building itself was likened to something out of a Charles Dickens book. Long before its closure in 1967 it had been condemned, but repairs and improvements lengthened its life considerably.

In 1964 the Scottish Education Department authorised the sum of £755 000 for School projects in Edinburgh, some of which was to be used to erect a replacement building. The money was not forthcoming that year, but in 1965 a sum of £65 000 was put forward as the estimated cost of a new school. Again the promises were not affordable and, in 1966, a group of parents lobbied the Education Department, demanding a new school in Tollcross to take the two hundred children on the roll.

The parents were informed that a new school in Tollcross was impossible as a suitable site was simply not available. The short term solution to relieve the overcrowding was then to teach the five to seven year olds at St Peter's Annexe behind St Thomas of Aquin's School in Chalmers Street. In the meantime St Peter's School in Falcon Avenue was being extended and in 1967 the four classes still at Glen Street were transferred, leaving the empty school to await its demolition.

St John's Episcopal School (18)

Situated at the corner of West Tollcross and Earl Grey Street was this mission school connected to St John's Episcopal Church at the West End. It was probably built in the late 1850s. In 1896 the Town Council purchased the Mission by compulsory order so that they could widen the road giving access to the proposed Tram Depot. The land which was left was sold to the Methodist Church.

Although the School did not continue, Mission work moved to St Kentigern's Church and hall at St Peter's Place.

St Thomas of Aquin's (19)

In the thirteenth century King James of Aragon bestowed upon the Order of Mercy—formed to ransom captives from the Moors—the right to use his coat of arms. To this day, with some heraldic changes, this coat of arms is still used in the school badge of St Thomas of Aquin's, along with the school motto: *Sit Nobiscum Deus* (Let God Be With Us).

In 1858 the Sisters of Mercy set up a Convent in Lauriston Gardens, dedicated to St Catherine of Sienna. In 1887 they founded St Catherine's Convent Boarding and Day School for Young Ladies at 6 Chalmers Street, the predecessor of St Thomas's. In 1900 this school extended to numbers 4–18 Chalmers Street where it remains to this day.

The new school was additionally a pupil-teacher centre. In 1905 there were thirty-five pupils and fifty pupil teachers, the latter trained solely for teaching the many poor children in the district. They began their training at the age of fourteen and, once qualified could attend the Roman Catholic Training College in Glasgow.

On 23 June 1905 a letter from the School was sent to the Education Department asking that it be recognised under the Continuation Code. After much consultation in 1906 the School was formerly entered onto the Department's records as Edinburgh St Thomas of Aquin's Higher Grade RC School.

In 1928 the Primary School was built beyond the playground which contained seven classrooms and two sewing rooms. For a time in the 1960s it was used to teach the infants of St Ignatius School in Glen Street. In 1967 it was referred to as St Peter's Annexe when the Glen Street School closed and moved to St Peter's School in Falcon Avenue. It is now used by the Secondary School.

St Thomas's has excelled in many avenues over the years. One of the proudest traditions built up by the Music Club was their reputation for singing the Gregorian Chant. In 1952 the club also distinguished itself in the open Scots Song section of the Edinburgh Festival of Music. Today, Music is still a very important part of the curriculum.

1952 was also a good year for the 15–18 year old netball when players won that section of the Scottish Netball Championships, and for many years Netball was the major sport at the school.

At the turn of the following decade St Thomas's was extensively reconstructed and refurbished, during which time pupils were 'boarded out' to other Schools. It reopened in 1961.

In August 1975 St Thomas's became a coeducational school; the 676 girls were joined for the first time by ninety boys.

In 1987 the school celebrated its centenary, and what better tribute could have been made than to the Sisters of Mercy who, through their valuable work, played such an important part in the development of the school we know today.

Tollcross Public School (20)

Tollcross Primary School, as it is now known, was built in 1912, on the site of the former Municipal Slaughterhouse on Fountainbridge, which in turn was partly on the grounds of the former Lochrin Distillery, owned by the Haig family. It replaced Lothian Road School, demolished to make way for the Usher Hall.

While the school was being built there was much controversy about the magnificent Slaughterhouse gates which had been erected in 1851 by David Cousin, the City Architect. In the many letters to the newspapers it was suggested that the gate should remain as a front entrance to the new school. At the time, Fountainbridge was being widened and the school was deliberately set back from the road. To retain the gates they would have needed to be moved. Unfortunately it was agreed to remove them altogether and the author has been unable to trace what happened to them.

Of all the interesting and industrious developments at the School, one that will be remembered by a generation of children is the aviary which was set up in 1969 by the Headmaster, George Baxter. It was to be found at the top of the first landing on the east side of the School, but there were no birds to fill it. After a letter to the *Evening News* the School was inundated with a wide variety of birds and books on how to look after them. Such was the interest that the children began making breeding boxes!

By 1984 the School roll had fallen to around 150 children, roughly a sixth of its full capacity. In response to a ten year campaign for a Community Centre in Tollcross, part of the ground floor was converted to accommodate this facility. Mr Gordon McRae, the Head Teacher at the time, will be remembered for the support and guidance he gave to the centre, which opened in March 1985. One of the groups based at the Centre is the Local History Project. Of interest to the other members of the Project and to the School Janitor is that his house, situated close to the school, is all that remains of the slaughterhouse buildings.

Torphichen Street School (21)

At the corner of Torphichen Street and Canning Street this school was opened in 1889 under the aegis of the Edinburgh School Board. It was staffed by ten assistant and six pupil teachers for a roll of 350 children, rising to 581 in 1932 when it ceased to be a day school. In 1898 it had also been an evening school for young women and girls. Above the entrance at Torphichen Street one can still see the sign 'Boys' and, at Canning Street 'Girls'.

In 1932 it became known as Torphichen Street Commercial Institute in response to the growing demands of businesses requiring better trained cleri-

Fig 6.5: Entrance to the New Greyfriars' School in 1914. It was once known as the Vennel Ragged Feeding School.

cal staff who had recently left school, learning English, typing, shorthand, hygiene, general office practice, and later social studies, on a day release basis further to polish up their skills.

The Institute had previously been located at West Fountainbridge School in 1918, nearly opposite Grove Street. However, it had originally started in a one roomed building in Grove Street. One of the staff employed at Fountainbridge from its inception was a Miss Gracie Allan, who taught book-keeping, shorthand and typing and also started classes for discharged disabled soldiers after the war. She transferred to Torphichen Street in 1932 and, when she retired in 1964, was the longest serving teacher in further education.

The Vennel Ragged Feeding School (22)
Founded in 1843 by the Revd Dr Robertson of New Greyfriars Church, the Vennel Ragged School relied heavily on voluntary contributions and legacies to survive. Although it received £185 annually from government grants, and £15 in fees from the Parochial Board, its annual expenditure was around £670.

Income was also found from charges made for the child's education. An annual sum of £2.10s helped to pay the teachers' salaries and to provide an efficient elementary education (with breakfast and dinner) for approximately 270 children.

It was hoped that the free meals provided would be an incentive to the parents to see that their children attended school regularly. But so destitute were the parents that they thought nothing of keeping the children away from school on the off chance they might earn a little money running messages and such like.

At a minimal cost clothing was also supplied. The School was greatly indebted to the individuals and associations for their gifts of materials and to the voluntary work of the ladies who made up the children's clothes.

By 1870 the school was referred to as New Greyfriars School and probably closed early this century.

Further reading

1 Cant, Malcolm, (1984). *Marchmont in Edinburgh.*
2 Edinburgh District Council, City of, Libraries Division (1986). *No Ordinary Man: Journal of William Anderson, 1902–06.*
3 Forbes Gray, W, (1935). *An Eighteenth Century Riding School.* BOEC, **20**.
4 Grant, James, (1882). *Old and New Edinburgh.*
5 Law, Alexander, (1965). *Education in Edinburgh in the Eighteenth Century.*
6 Simpson, W Douglas, (1962). *George Heriot's Hospital,* BOEC, **31**.
7 Smith, Charles J, (1978). *Historic South Edinburgh: Volume 1.*
8 Towill, Edwin W, (1956). *The Minutes of the Merchant Maidens' Hospital.* BOEC, **29**.

7

Churchgoing

Catherine Toall

Introduction

Again in this chapter it is not our intention, nor would it be possible, to offer a history of the various Church movements over the past few centuries. Some attempt has been made to show the origins or the physical movements of particular congregations, but for the most part a description of the Churches only is offered.

However, from the information given, it is possible to gain some understanding of the underlying differences between the Churches, how they functioned and what other activities they were involved with, apart from worship. In particular, the Free Church Movement is of interest since a great number of the Churches in the area were either built under this denomination or broke away from the Church of Scotland in 1843. It is of great interest that Thomas Chalmers, leader of the Disruption, actually founded and preached in a Church in the West Port in 1844, called Dr Chalmers Territorial Free Church.

One of the purposes of this evangelical movement was to build as many churches as possible to encourage churchgoing at a time when church seating space was limited, churchgoing not very widespread, and social deprivation acute.

This expansion also took place in other denominations but, overall, including the Free Church, the actual number of churchgoers did not increase substantially in the latter half of the nineteenth century. However, by 1851, after a great deal of building work throughout Scotland, there were seats for sixty-three per cent of the population.

In 1988, the number of churchgoers in the area is a fraction of what it was one hundred years ago (not least because of the steep decline in the local population). The number of Churches still open is also in small proportion to those described here (about one third); the Barclay Church, St John's, St Cuthbert's, the Sacred Heart, St Mark's, Viewforth, St Michael and All Saints, Gilmore Place Presbyterian, and the Methodist Central Hall are all that remain.

Most of the others have been demolished or, in the case of Lauriston Place

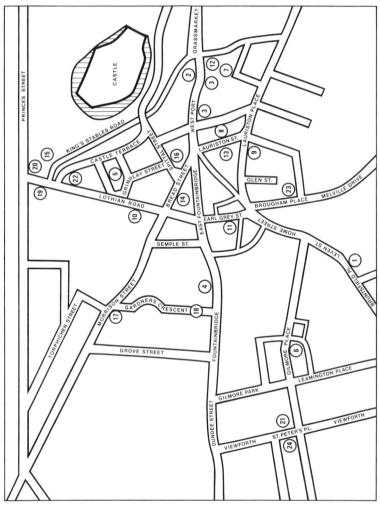

Fig 7.1: Map of the area showing where the churches were and are located.

Church and St Kentigern's, lying idle. Others have been put to other uses. For example Lothian Road Church now functions as the Filmhouse and, what was originally the Gaelic Church in Cambridge Street, has been converted into the Little Lyceum Theatre. The map shows where to find the Churches within the area.

Churches

The Barclay Church (1)
Architecturally, the Barclay Church is one of the most interesting in Edinburgh, if not in Scotland. Cleverly positioned in the old village of Wright's Houses it dominates the landscape from the Meadows and towers above the road to Bruntsfield, each side showing off new aspects to its intricate design.

It was the Free Church Presbytery in the mid nineteenth century who chose the site of the new church which was designed by the Edinburgh architrect F T Pilkington. To pay for the Church the Presbytery used £10 000 bequested for this purpose by Miss Mary Barclay. However, it was to cost nearly half as much again on its completion in 1864, two years after the foundation stone was laid.

The congregation over this period managed to raise £3000 to defray the building costs but another £1000 was needed to build an internal roof to protect against noise and draughts. The congregation were again quick to rally and the work was carried out. The original ceiling was painted blue and adorned with stars.

As the builders neared completion of the Church the Minister, Dr James Wilson, along with some of the office-bearers of the congregation and four of the masons, climbed to the top of the tower and gave thanks to God that the Church had been completed without loss of life or limb.

The same Minister had also been persuasive enough to have cancelled from the Pilkington's design several ornate angels which were to have adorned the roof. He was adament that the Church was there for worship and that it should not vulgarise religious symbols. Considering the grandiose style of the Church architecture one would not have thought the angels would have made much difference.

The Church has always shown an interest in both home and foreign missions. Early in its history the congregation built a Mission in West Fountainbridge and paid for the salary of the Missionary and the upkeep of the building. In 1873 the Church welcomed the American evangelical singers and preachers D L Moody and I D Sankey, who were touring Scotland that year. They spent their first week in Edinburgh at the Church.

Chapel of the Blessed Virgin Mary (2)
Certainly one of the oldest known churches in the area, situated between the West Port and the King's Stables, it was built in the fourteenth century and demolished in 1788. This little Chapel was used by the priest for the purposes of taking oaths on the gospels in the attestation of truth between participants in personal disputes, or to be on hand to administer last rites when required.

Further to the west of this Chapel was another, dedicated to Our Lady of Lorretto, about which little is known. The lane leading from the West Port to King's Stables Road was later called Lady Wynd. The parallel lane further to the east, adjacent to the Chapel of the Blessed Virgin Mary was called Chapel Wynd.

Chalmers Church (3)

Originally called Dr Chalmers Territorial Free Church and situated in the West Port, it was founded by Thomas Chalmers who was the leader of the Disruption of the Church of Scotland movement in 1843.

Around this time Dr Chalmers commissioned a census of 411 families in the West Port and found that 296 of these had no church connections and that 290 children had no access to education. Consequently Chalmers set up, in the autumn of 1844, a Church and School in a disused Tannery next to the old West Port Church which had been closed through ill repair. By the spring of 1845 the Tan Loft was filled to its capacity to hear Dr Chalmers preach in the morning. Such was Dr Chalmers popularity that his assistant minister William Tasker could only expect a handful of worshippers in the afternoon. However, by 1847, as attendance steadily increased and the work of the Church had prospered by his hand, William Tasker was ordained minister of the West Port Church when it moved into the refurbished Old Church at Johnston's Land, a tenement building numbered 32–34 West Port.

The old Church was certainly not built for comfort. The seats were narrow and the backs were straight and high. The pews were all provided with doors which were fastened with a snib, presumably in fear of absconders! The snibs seemed to have worked because the membership steadily increased to one thousand and it was becoming necessary to consider the building of a new and larger church.

This new church, built at the corner of the West Port and Lady Lawson Street, was designed by Hippolyte Blanc, the well-known Edinburgh architect, and was opened for worship in 1884. According to the Church records the attendance at the first service was 1442 and the collection amounting to £285, at that time a large sum of money.

The old Church was sold in 1930 and the proceeds were used to build the Chalmers Hall. The new Church was demolished in the 1970s and the site became a car park for the Art College. The old Church, although disused for a good number of years, stood until 1988 when it was demolished in April of that year.

Fountainbridge Church (4)

Fountainbridge Church was built in 1848 by St George's Free Church which, at that time was housed in a brick building at the foot of Lothian Road. It was referred to as Fountainbridge Mission until 1854 when it was sanctioned by the General Assembly as a full ministerial church.

In the mid nineteenth century Fountainbridge was an area of squalor, where Public Houses were plentiful and well patronised. No wonder that James Wilson, the first missionary, confessed that it was the hardest task of the many he had had to cope with. However hard it was, within ten years he had secured a membership of 1200.

Wilson was instrumental in setting up Kitchen meetings, Temperance Societies and Slaughterhouse services. He established a special Sunday evening service for people in 'working garb' which cause the church sometimes to be called the 'Moleskin Kirk'.

In 1920 the church was raised to full status and from its own congregation the first elders were appointed. In 1954, in its centenary year, the church was extensively renovated and the conical spire removed. The building was demolished in the 1970s.

The Gaelic Church (5)
The building now occupied by the Little Lyceum Theatre in Cambridge Street was originally called the Gaelic Church and was opened in 1851 by Dr R S Candlish.

Its history goes back to the aftermath of the 1745 rebellion when, after the break-up of the hereditary legal authority of the Highland chiefs, many clan members became soldiers in Scottish regiments. There were so many gaelic speaking soldiers stationed at Edinburgh Castle that the garrison chaplains undertook divine services. A chapel was set up in the Castle Wynd and the Revd Joseph Robertson MacGregor became the first minister.

When the Disruption of the Church of Scotland took effect in 1843 one of its leaders, the Revd James Noble, led nearly all of the gaelic speaking congregation away from the Castle Wynd chapel and set up a unit of the Free Church from a building in Castle Terrace known as the 'Brick Church', which was rented from St George's Church which had removed to Lothian Road in 1834. In 1864 the name of the church changed to St Columba's United Free Church.

By the turn of the century further division in the Church weakened the gaelic speaking church in Edinburgh. In 1892 a large number of the members joined the Free Presbyterian Church. In 1900 further division occurred and judicial proceedings followed claims to the Gaelic Church property. For a year and a half the congregation worshipped in Drumsheugh Gardens until it was restored at St Columba's.

The section of the population which had remained with the Church of Scotland after the Disruption joined with St Columba's in 1948 and the church changed its name once again to the Highland Church. At this time within the Church of Scotland it was the only church which preached in the 'old mother tongue'.

In 1956 after a great deal of controversy the Highland Church joined with the Burgh Church of Tolbooth St John's at the top of Johnston Terrace. The building has now been converted into a Heritage Centre.

Gilmore Place United Presbyterian Church (6)
The congregation of this church came from Portsburgh Associate Presbyterian Congregation Church in the Vennel. Built at a cost of £7900 it first opened its doors in April 1881.

Fig 7.2: Graham Street Synagogue in 1914. It was originally New Greyfriars' Free Church.

Graham Street Synagogue (7)

This church originated in the former Ross House in Park Place, off Teviot Row. The building was transformed into a house of worship where it remained until 1896. Park Place was completely demolished by that date because of expansion of Edinburgh University and no longer exists.

By 1898 the congregation of Greyfriars Free Church in Graham Street had vacated its premises and a new Synagogue was set up in its place, the first Rabii being the Revd Moses Joel.

The congregation remained there until 1932 when, along with another two congregations in the City, combined to form the new Synagogue in Salisbury Road.

The West side of Graham Street, where the Synagogue stood, and the north side of Keir Street were bought by the Art College and were demolished. The east side of Graham Street is now called Keir Street.

Lady Lawson Street Church (8)

The Church was situated on the West side of Lady Lawson Street and was probably built in the mid eighteenth century. It appears on an improvement plan of 1791, illustrated in Chapter I.

In 1835 the Church was rebuilt and was described then as a Reformed

Presbyterian Congregation Church. Later in 1852 it appeared on the Ordnance Survey map as a Secessionist Church.

It is not known when it was demolished and the site is now a car park
opposite the Art College.

Lauriston Church (9)
The congregation of this Church originated in the Nicolson Street General
Associate Church around 1786. It then moved to Portsburgh Church built
in 1808 part of the congregation of which moved to the existing, though now
unused, building at the corner of Lauriston Place and Gardens, built in 1859.

In 1900 the church was incorporated into the United Free Church of
Scotland and in 1929 into the Church of Scotland. After its closure in 1980
the congregation moved to the Barclay Church.

Lothian Road Church (10)
Lothian Road Church started out in 1831 as a United Associate Congregation
which had previously worshipped at Gardeners' Hall Church which then
became St David's Church (Gardner's Crescent).

The first Minister of the congregation in 1828 was the Revd David Marr
who died at the early age of thirty-seven in the year 1834. Before his death
the Church was in great debt and, either through extremely good foresight
or for some other unknown reason, the Church insured the life of Mr Marr
for £999.19s with the Caledonian Insurance Company only months before
he died.

The Church had a long and interesting history, far greater than could be
reiterated here. It closed in 1976, the congregation transferring to Palmerston
Place. The Church was then converted into the Filmhouse Cinema in 1978,
expanding its facilities to include a second cinema, a booking office, foyer and
bar and restaurant in 1982, under the trusteeship of Paul Getty Jnr and Bell's
Scotch Whisky.

Methodist Central Hall (11)
The history of this Church and hall goes back to 1766 when John Wesley's
own Octagonal Church was built in the Calton area of Edinburgh, demolished
to make way for the General Post Office at the East End of Princes Street.

The congregation moved to Nicolson Square Church in 1815 and, when
in the 1880s overcrowding forced them to move to larger premises, they
moved into temporary premises at the Albert Hall in Shandwick Place. In
1890 however, when an Exhibition in Edinburgh attracted thousands of
visitors and, after advertising there a series of four sermons, the Albert Hall
became crowded to excess. Hastily the office bearers secured the larger premises of the Synod Hall in Castle Terrace, then owned by the United Presbyterian
Church, but previously a theatre. Its 2000 person capacity was entirely
adequate for the newly enlarged congregation and it remained there for
eleven years.

In the meantime the Methodist Church was keen to secure a good site for
the building of a new church. At the turn of the twentieth century they were

lucky enough to have the support of the then City Engineer in the purchase of the land at the corner of Earl Grey Street. The city had bought the land from St John's Episcopal School by compulsory purchase in order to widen the road for greater access to the new tram depot in West Tollcross. It was to cost around £53 000, an inflated sum due to the financial failure of the initial contractor. It was finally opened in 1901 for the dedicatory Service by the Revd George Jackson, the founder and first Superintendent.

The cost of building this magnificent building was defrayed from rents received from the shop premises on Earl Grey Street, from the Methodists' Twentieth Century organisation and from public collections and individual subscriptions.

The Central Hall is noted for its patronage of various activities organised by the congregation, as well as recreational, educational and cultural groups meeting there, and was instrumental in the setting up of Crosswinds Community Centre sponsored by the Tollcross Council of Churches and the Regional Council Community Education Service.

At the time of writing the Central Hall is having its stonework cleaned, revealing the interesting and unusual pink tinged sandstone, which will highlight the original Glasgow Art Nouveau glass windows.

Portsburgh Church (12)

This Church was built in 1808 as the first established church of the General Associate Congregation of Nicholson Street. It survived until the late nineteenth century when it was converted into part of a Salvation Army Women's Hostel. It was probably built on the site of the Portsburgh Meeting Place of the seventeenth and eighteenth century.

Sacred Heart Church (13)

Although this Church has ancient roots in the Society of Jesus, founded by Ignatius Loyola in 1540, it was not until 1859 that the Parish of Lauriston was set up to satisfy the needs of some of the 15 000–20 000 Catholics in Edinburgh at the time. The first Chapel was only a temporary measure in converted premises in the east Grassmarket at Hunter's Close. On the Feast of St Ignatius (31 July 1859), the foundation stone of the new Church was laid and the Parish dedicated to the Most Sacred Heart of Jesus.

Also in the same year a Parish School was opened at Hunter's Close, and in the next year further premises were acquired at Brown's Close. St Ignatius School as it was known, removed to Glen Street in 1864. The new Church in Lauriston Street opened in July of 1860.

It would seem by the turn of the century that the Catholic voice was not listened to very readily in Edinburgh. A newspaper article of 1903 represents the zeal with which Father Power tried to increase its volume:

> For the past few years Father Power, one of the Jesuit Fathers attached to the Mission of the Sacred Heart, Lauriston, has conducted open air services on Sunday evenings of the summer months. He preached firstly in the Grassmarket but latterly he was to be seen standing among large crowds in Lothian Road.

The spot where he usually takes up his stand is marked by a large wooden cross. . . Last night a crowd of a thousand people listened for more than an hour.

The intervening history of this Church would take up many more pages. Suffice it to say that the author, while not a Catholic herself, recalls the high esteem in which the Brothers were held and the important part the Church played and still plays in the community. A story which sums her feelings up occurred earlier this century when a School Inspector visited a class at St Ignatius School in Glen Street and asked 'Who is the Head of the Catholic church?' and was astonished to receive the unanimous reply, 'Please Father, Brother Holden!'

St Aidan's Church (14)

This Church was built in 1880 as a Chapel of Relief of the United Presbyterian Church of St Cuthbert's congregation. It was situated 150 yards along from Lothian Road on the south side of Bread Street and was approached by steps leading to its entrance.

It is known that St Cuthbert's Cooperative bought the Church in 1934 converting it into an extension to the central drapery department, until it was demolished just before the Second World War.

St Cuthbert's Church (15)

According to tradition the first church to be built on the site of the present church, if not built by the personal effort of St Cuthbert himself, was at least built shortly after he died in AD 687. Throughout its early history among the numerous religious foundations belonging to or connected with the West Kirk (as it was later to be known) prior to the Reformation, were the Chapel of the Blessed Virgin Mary, the Chapel of Our Lady of Lorretto (both in Wester Portsburgh) and the Chapels of St Roque's and St John's (both situated on the Burgh Muir).

During the sixteenth century it must have suffered greatly from damage because of the frequent sieges of the Castle by the English Army. Having then only a thatched roof it was certainly not a robust building. Rather than renovating the Church it was decided in 1593 to erect a second Church, known as the 'Little Kirk' which stood until the middle to the seventeenth century.

It is highly unlikely that the Church was not rebuilt several times over between AD 678 and 1773 when there is a well documented description of its demolition. Indeed evidence of at least five distinct foundations were discovered at this time. Also discovered and documented at this time is a rather macabre but fascinating finding:

The workmen, in digging away the rubbish at the West Kirk, Edinburgh, which is to be rebuilt, discovered lately a leaden coffin, which contained some bones, and a leaden urn. Upon opening the urn, a most fragrant smell issued out. On inspecting the cause of it, they found a human heart finely embalmed, and in the highest state of perfection. No inscription was upon the coffin by which the

THE OLD CHURCH OF S⊤ CUTHBERT AND NORTH LOCH EDINBURGH.

Fig 7.3: A print of the Old Church of St Cuthbert viewed from the North Loch around 1774. The North Loch was drained and is now Princes Street Gardens.

date could be traced, but it must have been there for some centuries. It is conjectured that the heart belonged to some person, who, in the time of the crusades, had gone to the Holy Land, and been there killed, and the heart, as was customary in those times, embalmed, and sent home to be interned with some of the family.

Apart from being in a ruinous and irreparable condition, another compelling reason for a new church was the large increase of population in Edinburgh in the latter half of the eighteenth century. It was built in 1775 by a succession of architects, one of whom was James Weir of Tollcross, who designed the canopied pulpit, the double gallery and, probably, its high box pens.

However, by 1892 this structure had become old fashioned and inadequate for a congregation which was reckoned to be one of the largest in Scotland. Accordingly between 1892 and 1894 the present structure was erected at the cost of £50 000.

St Cuthbert's United Free Church (16)
Built in the mid nineteenth century in Spittal Street, the Church was sold in 1911 for £2500 to the Tuberculosis Trust to create the Royal Victoria Dispensary. Still having a church-like feel to it, it is now an X-Ray centre. Both St Cuthbert's Free Church and Greyfriars' Free Church (see Graham Street Synagogue) had a mission at Riego Street at the turn of the century.

Fig 7.4: The St Cuthbert's (United) Free and Greyfriars' Free Church Mission, Riego Street, in 1914. Riego Street no longer exists as a through road.

St David's Church (off Morrison Street) (17)
St David's Church was set up as a Free Church from a Church of Scotland congregation at St David's Parish Church in Gardner's Crescent, formerly Gardeners' Hall Church. It was built in 1844. Between 1843 and 1844 the congregation had worshipped both in a tent and in the Royal Riding Academy in Lothian Road. It was built in a Nursery garden and was surrounded by tenements towards the turn of the century.

It closed in 1961 and united with Broomhouse church.

St David's Church (Gardner's Crescent) (18)
W S Gardner owned the land upon which Gardner's Crescent was built. Before the street was laid there was a large house called Gardeners' Hall at the Morrison Street end of the lands and Gardeners' Hall Church near Fountanbridge. Built in 1826 a congregation of the Secession body worshipped there until 1831 when it moved to Lothian Road Church. Gardeners' Hall Church was then sold to the Church of Scotland who renamed it St David's Parish Church.

The Church was demolished at the turn of the century to make Gardner's Crescent a through road for traffic to Fountainbridge. Previously pedestrian access only could make its way under the canal by way of a tunnel.

The congregation moved to Viewforth Church.

Fig 7.5: On the right of these cottages on Fountainbridge is a passageway with an overhead sign reading 'St David's Parish Church'. It stood at the head of Gardner's Crescent until the new road was built connecting it with Fountainbridge in the 1920s.

St George's Chapel (19)

The history of St George's in Lothian Road goes back first to what was known as the 'Brick Church' in Castle Terrace and prior to that in a chapel in Charlotte Square.

Described as a brick building of Gothic architecture it was designed by David Bryce in 1834. It was in the same year, after serving only a few weeks as assistant, that the Revd Dr R S Cavendish became Minister.

In 1843 the Church left the body of the Church of Scotland to become a Free Church and as for the rest of its life was referred to as 'Dr Candlish's Church'.

In 1866 an agreeable offer was made by the Caledonian Railway Company who wanted to extend their terminus to Princes Street. The Free Church sold the land and built Free St George's West on Shandwick Place.

St John's Church (20)

The congregation of this Episcopalian Church began in the late eighteenth century with an invitation to the Revd Daniel Sandford from Surrey and first worshipped in a hall in West Register Street. It then had built a new church for its own purposes in Charlotte Square in 1802. However, this church was too small for a growing church-going population and a new site was found at the west end of Princes Street, although not without opposition from the city fathers.

The Church was near completion in 1818 when Edinburgh was hit by a ferocious storm and part of the tower was blown down. Two massive ornamental stones fell through the roof and floor of the Church into the vaults below. Despite the extra costs the building work was renovated within two months and was consecrated by Bishop Sandford, as he had then become.

The first few years of the Church's history were not without controversy. In 1819 the organist was dismissed after complaints about his poor musical abilities. As great were complaints about how cold the Church was. Worse still, by 1822, the Church had got into heavy debt. However, by 1834 after the Church gained grounds for burials it was able to make good profits from selling plots.

Although later in the nineteenth century and into the first quarter of the twentieth century money had again become a problem, the Church was able to sell off land to the City so that it could widen both the junction at Princes Street, and Lothian Road itself.

In recent times, with backing of the Council of West End Churches, St John's converted the vaults below into the Cornerstone Cafe, and later, next to it, a bookshop. The Justice and Peace Centre has for a number of years occupied the premises and regularly paints stunning and often highly provocative murals concerning world issues, such as racism and totalitarianism.

St Kentigern's (21)

When in 1896 the Town Council bought by compulsory purchase order the land at the corner of Earl Grey Street and West Tollcross to widen the road, St John's Episcopal School and Mission had to close.

Rather than build another school it was decided to build a Church and hall in St Peter's Place. It was designed by Dick Peddie and called St Kentigern's. The foundation stone was laid in December 1897.

The church was closed in 1941 and the premises were leased to the town which turned it into a children's nursery. Pupils from Darroch School often were placed there as part of the school curriculum.

Sadly forlorn looking, with its windows bricked up, the Church still stands on the banks of the Union Canal. It was approached through a pend under the tenement in St Peter's Place, which is now locked up. One can still see the signs saying 'St Kentigern's—all seats free'!

St Mark's Unitarian Church (22)

The Unitarian congregation in Edinburgh traces its origins back to the time of the Covenanters, one branch of whom formed themselves into the Secessionist movement in Berwickshire. In 1776 some members of the group came to Edinburgh and established a Secessionist society, which by 1813 became known as the Unitarian Church.

In 1835 they built the Church which still stands in Castle Terrace today, designed by the prolific David Bryce, who had also shaped St George's Church and Lothian Road Church.

St Michael and All Saints' Church (23)

Up until the building of this Episcopal Church in Brougham Street in 1867, which at that time was called the Church of All Saints, the congregation had worshipped in St John's Mission Hall at the corner of Earl Grey Street and West Tollcross.

Early in 1965 St Michael's Episcopal Church in Hill Square was closed and its congregation united with that of All Saints.

Taken from St Michael's later that year were the relics of St Francis of Sales and St Catherine of Sienna which were entombed in the High Altar of All Saints by the Rt Revd Bishop Kenneth Carey.

Viewforth Church (24)

Also known as Viewforth, St David and St Oswald, it was originally St Peter's Free Church, the congregation of which came from Fountainbridge Church in 1871. Beneath the Church there was a school room and vestry.

The total cost of the building work was £4500, of which £1300 was used to build the 120 feet high spire. Although the Church is still in excellent condition, the tower was removed in 1976.

Further reading

1 Balfour-Melville, E W M, (1959). *A Short History of the Church of St John the Evangelist.*
2 Forbes Gray, W, (1948). *Historic Churches of Edinburgh.*
3 Mitchell, Alex H, (1911). *The History of Lothian Road United Free Church Congregation.*
4 Smout, T C, (1986). *A Century of the Scottish People 1830–1950.*

8

The Local Streets

Drew Easton

Introduction

The reasons why streets in Edinburgh were so named have seldom been recorded. We have to rely to a great extent on interpretation and imaginative guesswork, although much of what we know about the names can be construed from the notes of the late Charles Boog Watson, who collected a vast amount of the supporting evidence which is used in this chapter. We have attempted here to expand upon his and other people's findings, but the derivations of some names are still unknown.

One of the most frustrating of these is Bread Street, so-named around 1823. Boog Watson thought that there may have been a Bread Society on this street but, according to the Master Baker's Association, such societies did not own premises at this time, tending to meet in one another's houses. Others have guessed that there were many bakeries in the area but in the Street Directory of the time only one has been recorded.

Bread Street changed from its original name of Orchardfield when the Merchant Company was developing the lands northwards of its position to Castle Terrace and Lothian Road. The first tenement at number 1 to 33 was built at this time but the Company's records give no hint at all which could help to solve the puzzle. Other leads have been followed but it remains open to future enthusiasts to come up with a good answer to this enquiry.

Bread Street is a comparatively recent name. One of the earliest is Drum-dryan, which is of Celtic origin and others like the High Riggs are of mediaeval times. Many refer to notable people of their time, few of whom had any relationship to the area. Occasionally we find evidence that a name has been changed, for whatever reason, and some that had been planned with one name in mind but which never actually received the honour.

One danger in looking at maps for clues is discovering streets which appear to have disappeared through time. Sometimes this is the case (eg Freer Street, off Fountainbridge) but mostly they were only planned and never actually laid. Grove Street Square was one example. A complex series of streets at the Sheraton Hotel site was another, perhaps scrapped because of competition for land in favour of the Caledonian Railway Company in the 1840s.

Fig 8.1: This tenement at 1–19 Barclay Place is an excellent example of late Victorian Gothic, struggling to live beside the imposing architecture of the Barclay Church.

Rationalisation of street names over the last century has caused many names to disappear. In the 1960s many names in common to Leith and Edinburgh were sorted out to avoid confusion. Graham Street at Lauriston was one to go in favour of its Leith counterpart. Morrison Street at one time only referred to the length of road from Haymarket to Dewar Place but has now replaced a whole host of named streets up to Lothian Road.

So, with caution in mind, the following derivations are offered, along with snippets of topographical interest which did not find a place in other chapters.

Admiral Terrace
Named after Admiral Peat who lived in Viewforth House in the mid nineteenth century. Boroughmuir School now stands on the site of the house and grounds.

Archibald Place
Built on the grounds of a Nursery Garden owned by George Archibald in the early nineteenth century.

Barclay Place, Terrace
In memory of a Miss Mary Barclay who provided most of the funds to build the Barclay Church.

The outstanding tenements at Nos 1–19 Barclay Place were built in 1885 by Thomas P Marwick and often go unnoticed, except by those who live in Gillespie Crescent.

Barrace Steps
To be found between the Castle Terrace Car Park and the King's Bridge in commemoration of the mediaeval Barras (tilting ground) described in Chapter I.

Belfrage Lane
After Andrew Belfrage who built a tenement between the High Riggs and Lauriston Place in 1826. Houses in this area were demolished in the mid 1960s to make way for Goldberg's Department Store.

Brandfield Street
When Sir Alexander Brand bought the mansion and lands of Dalry in 1696 he changed their name to Brandsfield, (see Chapter I). Other streets in the area were likewise called Brandfield Place and Gardens but were incorporated into Fountainbridge and demolished through expansion of the Fountain Brewery earlier this century. Only two stairs remain in this street as a consequence of this expansion.

Bread Street, Street Lane
Renamed from Orchardfield to Bread Street in 1823, there is no known explanation of the name. The only baker in the street before and after the change was a William Gray. No evidence has been found of a Bread Society reputed to have met at premises in this street. Before tenements numbered 1–33 were built around this time there were very few buildings. The Orchardfield estate (see Chapter I) was being developed during this period which would account for the number of building companies on the south side of the street towards the Main Point.

Brougham Place, Street
Named after Lord Henry Brougham, Statesman, in the 1820s. Until 1859, when Melville Drive was built, there were no houses on these streets. Henry Brougham was born in Edinburgh in 1778.

Brown's Place
By the Vennel this street was built around 1827 by James Brown, builder of stables and houses there.

Bruntsfield Place
Named after the lands of Brownsfield first owned by Richard Browne in 1381. The villas immediately below the Bruntsfield Hotel were built in 1826–7 and

for a long time were known as the 'Doctors' Houses' because of their medical practitioner residents. The Hotel was constructed from three double villas built in 1861–3.

Cambridge Street
Built in 1850 it was originally to be called Watson Street as it was built on land owned by George and John Grindlay who bequeathed part of the sale to George Watson's Hospital, now part of the Royal Infirmary. The name was changed to Cambridge after Queen Victoria's cousin, the Duke of Cambridge.

Castle Terrace
Facing the Castle, this roadway was laid in 1831 although No 1 was built around 1824. The outstanding tenement on the corner of Spittal Street and Castle Terrace was designed by James Gowans in 1868, who also designed the School Board Office, the Parish Council Building and the Synod Hall which were all demolished between 1965 and 1969. The gap site still remains in 1988 after nearly twenty years of argument about the merits of an Opera House for Edinburgh being built there.

Chalmers Buildings
Erected in 1855 next to Fountainbridge Church in honour of Dr Thomas Chalmers, a leader in the Disruption movement, giving rise to the Free Church of Scotland.

Chalmers Street
In honour of George Chalmers, plumber, who bequeathed a large sum of money to build Chalmers Hospital nearby.

Chapel Wynd
Situated off the West Port, the Chapel dedicated to the Blessed Virgin Mary, which stood between the Barras and King's Stables, was built in the fourteenth century and demolished in 1788. This little Chapel was used by the priest for the purposes of taking oaths on the gospels in the attestation of truth between participants in personal disputes, or to be on hand to administer last rites when required.

Cornwall Street
Originally intended to be named Erskine Street after Mary Erskine, pioneer in girls' education, who opened the Merchant Maidens' Hospital in Lauriston Place next to Watson's Hospital. Built in 1850 it was then named after the then Duke of Cornwall.

Dewar Place
Built around 1817 after a James Dewar, a mason living in Tobago Street, now off Morrison Street, immediately to the east of Dewar Place but originally part of Morrison Street.

The building now used as a Service Centre for the South of Scotland

Electricity Board was built in 1896 as the Electric Lighting Central Generating Station.

Dunbar Street
Appearing on Kirkwood's map of 1817 the street does not appear to have been named until the late 1820s. A sasine of 1830 refers to two acres of land belonging to Adam Paterson 'fronting the street now called Dunbar Street'. As yet no explanation of the name has been found. It is possible that it was originally called Wellington Place. There are no longer any houses on this street off West Tollcross.

Fig 8.2: Drumdryan House before it was demolished in 1959. The tenements at the rear are on the east side of Drumdryan Street and the path from the house leads to a pend in the tenement at Tarvit Street. The pend is still visible today.

Drumdryan Street

Named after the lands of Drumdryan, latterly owned by James Home Rigg whose property the road runs through. The name Drumdryan is Celtic in origin and denotes a row of Blackthorn trees.

Drumdryan House owned by Home Rigg was approached by a lane of the same name and was situated between Tarvit, Drumdryan and Brougham Street and latterly was surrounded by the existing tenements there until it was demolished earlier this century.

Earl Grey Street

Originally called and part of Lothian Road from 1788 to the early 1820s when its name was changed to Wellington Street in honour of the Duke of Wellington. In 1834 the name was changed to Earl Grey Street after Lord Grey, architect of the 1832 Parliamentary Reform Bill, who visited Edinburgh in that year.

The east side of the street was demolished in the 1970s for the purposes of widening the road.

Fig 8.3: A tenement in Fountainbridge built by F T Pilkington, who designed the Barclay Church. The tenements in Grove Street, adjacent to this one are also his work. It is not known why he elected to design this building but it is certainly one of the most unusual in Edinburgh.

Festival Square
In honour of the Edinburgh International Festival.

Filmhouse Lane
Named after the Filmhouse, formerly Lothian Road Church. It was previously
called St Antony's Place Lane. St Antony's Place is now part of Morrison
Street, from Semple Street to Lothian Road.

Fountainbridge
At the beginning of the eighteenth century the bridge which crossed the Dalry
Burn, flowing from the Burgh Loch (now the Meadows) to the Water of
Leith near Roseburn, situated nearly at the head of Grove Street, was called
'Foullbridge'. The river was called 'Foullburn', which at that time was a
common sewer. In St Cuthbert's Churchyard a headstone reads: 'Here lies
the body of Bailie Robert Mitchel, Portioner of Foull-Bridge, born 1667 and
died 1730'. After 1735 the name Fountainbridge became a more common
and better sounding alternative, naming the area after the Fountain or Well
nearly opposite Grove Street, the water from which was unpolluted. By 1773
most residences in the area were referred to in relation to the Fountain rather
than the bridge.

Gardner's Crescent
In 1821 a William Gardner WS bought the feu of the land and house called
Gardeners' Hall owned previously by the Society and Fraternity of Gardeners,
founded in 1722. William Gardner demolished the house situated at the north
end of the modern street and on its grounds had built the Crescent in 1822.

Gillespie Crescent, Place, Street
Named after James Gillespie who owned a Snuff Mill near Colinton at whose
bequest was built Gillespie's Hospital in the grounds of Wright's Houses (see
Chapter I). The Crescent was built at the end of the nineteenth century.
   The Royal Blind Asylum Workshops occupied the old Gillespie School
opposite the Crescent from 1925. Until the Second World War the workforce
was engaged in traditional handicrafts, but the work became more mechanised, making bedding and other wire work goods as well. During the 1950s
and 1960s their products became less competitive in the market and working
conditions were severely criticised by the National League for the Blind. It
was not until 1973 that the workshop moved to modern premises in Craig-
millar. The administration building remains on the grounds as does the shop
at No 1 Bruntsfield Place.

Gilmore Place (and Upper and Lower), Lane, Park, Upper Gilmore Terrace
Gilmore Street was constructed in 1798 through property owned by Samuel
Gilmore who owned a large ropemaking factory on the north side of Gilmore
Place, as it became known. He also owned the mansion house called Lochrin
Lodge whose entrance was on the north side of Home Street. He owned a
retail outlet at 100 Grassmarket.

In St Cuthbert's Churchyard a headstone commemorating several members of the Gilmore family suggests that the name Gilmore Place refers to the family rather than one individual:

> William Gilmore, rope manufacturer, Grassmarket (b 1809—d 1864), Samuel Gilmore (d 1812) and wife Elizabeth Gibson (d 1834)—William's father and mother.
> Samuel Gilmore, ropemaker (b 1739—d 1802)—Samuel's father, David Gilmore, late ropemaker (b 1740—d 1805)—Samuel's uncle.

Glen Street

Glen Street was built in 1870 after the last occupants of a large house and grounds, the sisters, the Misses Glen, daughters of Captain Nisbet Glen RN, who owned the property in the early nineteenth century. The periodical called *The Builder* described the tenements in 1869 as 'respectable'.

Glengyle Terrace

Probably named after Glengyle, home of the Clan McGregor. Named in honour of William and Duncan McGregor who owned the lands of Valleyfield in the mid nineteenth century. The street was built around 1869 on the grounds of Valleyfield House built in 1687, (see Chapter I).

Granville Terrace

Probably after 2nd Earl of Granville, Colonial Secretary 1868–1876 and Foreign Secretary in 1880.

Grindlay Street

After the brothers George and John Grindlay, Tanners, who owned the lands of Orchardfield (see Chapter I) on which the modern Street is situated. The Grindlay bequest on the sale of the lands went to the Merchant Company.

In St Cuthbert's Church a headstone reads:

> Mr John Grindlay, leather merchant in Edinburgh, who, mindful of the public charities of his native town, bequeathed the residue of his property equally to the Royal Infirmary, James Gillespies and the Orphan Hospitals of Edinburgh.
> Born 16 January 1781, died 9 August 1857.

Grove Street, Upper Grove Place

Near the top of Brandfield Street there stood a mansion built by Baron Kennedy in the early eighteenth century. By 1775 it was owned by Lord Colville who renamed it 'The Grove'. The property, which stretched from Fountainbridge to Morrison Street, was sold off into smaller areas from 1820 onwards.

As part of the Grove Street development an elaborate 'Grove Square' was planned but not realised.

Numbers 70 to 76 Grove Street were built around 1865 as a Working Men's Home which closed in 1987. The tenement was designed by Frederick T Pilkington, who also designed the Barclay Church. Round the corner at 158–164 Fountainbridge the equally intriguing tenement is also his work.

Hailes Street
Named after the Hailes estate where James Gillespie owned a Snuff Mill whose Trust owned the land upon which the street was built (see Gillespie Crescent).

Heriot Place
From George Heriot, Goldsmith, who left funds for the building of Heriot's Hospital built between 1628 and 1650, and later to become George Heriot's School, as it is today. The lands were previously called Heriot's Wark.

The remains of the wall surrounding the School were built after the Battle of Flodden in 1513, further to protect the Old Town from invasion.

High Riggs
Named after and forming the north west boundary of the lands of High Riggs with Tollcross. It was called variously Cowfeeder Row, Tollcross, Two-penny Custom and High Riggs throughout the late eighteenth century and early nineteenth century. By 1851 the street was split into sections including all of these names, with the addition of Hamilton Place. By the 1880s the whole length became established solely as the High Riggs.

Fig 8.4: The High Riggs in 1904. Most of the houses on the left of the picture were demolished before 1914.

Home Street
The 'artisan' tenements between Tarvit and Brougham Street were built around 1820 on land owned by James Home Rigg, wealthy shareholder of the Bank of Scotland, who lived in Drumdryan House nearby. Until the 1890s Home Street was situated only on the east side of the road and included Nos 1–17 inclusive at the lower end of what is now Lauriston Place.

Hopetoun Court
Named after Port Hopetoun the first canal basin on the Union Canal, where now stands Lothian House opposite. A tribute to Lord Hopetoun whose collieries in West Lothian were a major supplier of coal to Edinburgh, much of which came by canal after 1822.

Keir Street
Originally only between Heriot Place and Graham Street both connecting to Lauriston Place but now including Graham Street. Named after Adam Keir who owned land in this part of Lauriston near the turn of the eighteenth century. In 1782 his house is described as 'to be let, a large and commodious house and offices built by Mr Keir and now possessed by Mr Graham.'

King's Bridge
Built in 1827 in honour of King George IV who visited Edinburgh in 1822.

King's Stables Road, Lane
From the fourteenth century Royal stables built by David II immediately outwith the modern Grassmarket. This road was previously called 'the Road to Queensferry' before Lothian Road was built, and continued across the modern West End of Princes Street to Queensferry Road. King's Stables Lane was called Tanner Street in 1784.

Lady Lawson Street
Named after Lady Lawson, wife of Lord Robert Lawson of Hieriggs (High Riggs), who was Judiciary Clerk of James IV in 1493, this street was formerly known as Lady Lawson Wynd or Vennel. It originally lay only between Lauriston and West Port but was extended to Spittal Street after a Victorian Improvement Scheme.

Lady Wynd
This lane was named after a Chapel dedicated to Our Lady of Loretto, situated off the West Port.

Ladyfield Place
Thought to be after Lady Lawson but no evidence of this has been found.

Lauriston Place, Street, Terrace, Gardens, Park
The earliest map reference showing 'Lauriston' (Edgar 1765) shows the street running from modern day Forrest Road to the West Port by way of Lauriston

Street. Towards the close of the eighteenth century the Tollcross to Lauriston section appears as Lauriston Lane and later Portland Place and West Lauriston Place. Probably named after John Lowrie or Laurie who feued land in the area around 1566.

The newly renovated and cleaned tenements bounded by Keir Street and Heriot Place, now owned by the Lister Housing Cooperative were built between 1814 and 1832.

The old Fire Station was built in 1900 on part of the site of a Cattle Market which remained until 1910. In 1907 the College of Art was also built on the market grounds. Before the Fire Station was built much concern was expressed about the fire engines colliding into droves of cattle.

Leamington Terrace, Road
Possibly named after the English spa town of the same name. A neighbouring street Montpelier may be similarly named after the spa resort in France.

Leven Street, Terrace
These streets are named after Alexander, fifth Earl of Leven, who bought Drumdryan House in 1750 and renamed it Leven Lodge. It was pulled down in 1905 to make way for the King's Theatre.

Fig 8.5: Bennet's Bar, Leven Street, as it is today. The name Marshall, the original owner, appears both on the side wall and on the decorative glasswork inside.

Bennet's Bar by the King's Theatre is part of a tenement built in 1872. The superb original 'Jacobethan' interior is set off by tiled pictures by William B Simpson and Sons of London. In 1900 the proprietor of the pub was Robert Marshall. The name Marshall can still be seen on decorative glasswork within the public bar and on the outside wall next to the King's Theatre. On the pub's doorstep is the words 'Established in 1839' which may refer to a former business of the Marshall family.

Lochrin Buildings, Place, Lane, Terrace
Taken from the Dalry Burn which ran from the Burgh Loch (now the Meadows), across Home Street and Fountainbridge to the Water of Leith at Roseburn. The Loch was completely drained by 1812.

The area of Lochrin was previously called Newbigging and changed to Lochrin around 1756.

Lonsdale Terrace
Built in the late nineteenth century, the street was named after the famous Edinburgh Physician, Henry Lonsdale of the Royal Infirmary, who died in 1875. This street was laid out for planning in 1822, to be called Morton Crescent. It was to be a slightly different shape from the one chosen and was to have been in honour of James Home Rigg of Morton and Downfield, on whose lands the Crescent was built.

Lothian Road
Kay's Portraits (1877) tells the story of how the road was built in one day in 1785 for a bet and to the total disregard of house and property. There is no historical evidence to back up this story. The road originally applied to Earl Grey Street (built in 1788) as well and, in 1822 the stretch of road between Morrison Street and Fountainbridge was called Downie Place (after the Chairman of the Union Canal Company) until the basin was filled in in 1922.

Until the 1970s the Earl Grey section of the road was much narrower than the rest of Lothian Road. The latter had been widened on a number of occasions. A painting of around 1790 attributed to John Clerk of Edinburgh shows Lothian Road in its original state and is in the care of the National Galleries of Scotland.

Main Point, The
Formerly the 'Two-penny Custom', the first map reference is Kirkwood 1817 and refers to the main route to the town by way of the West Port, from the arterial roads of Lauriston Street, the High Riggs, East Fountainbridge and Bread Street.

The 'gushet' house on the corner of High Riggs and East Fountainbridge (Main Point House) was built around 1770 with purpose built shop below. The Public House frontage was added in 1897 and an extra storey in 1906.

Melville Drive
Named after a Lord Provost of Edinburgh, Sir John Melville, who opened the road in 1859.

The pillars on either side and at each end of Melville Drive were built in 1886 as part of the International Exhibition of Industry, Art and Science (see Chapter 8).

Morrison Street
When first built, this street ran from Haymarket to Dewar Place only, and was named after William Morrison, writer, of the late eighteenth century, whose lands were called Morrison Park. Sections of this street were previously called Grove Place, Rosehall Place, Rosemount, (part of) Orchardfield, Jamaica Street, Romilly Place and Street, Spence's Place, Tobago Street, Castlebarns and St Antony's Place, and have now been incorporated into the single named street. Originally it was called the Road to Falkirk.

Newport Street
Built in 1855 and named after the second basin of the Union Canal called Port Hamilton built in 1823 after Port Hopetoun. No houses remain on this street but it is due to be redeveloped in the late 1980s.

Old Hay Weight
The earliest reference to the Hay Weight (or steelyard) can be found on a feuing plan (see Chapter I) of 1791 as part of Dun's Stables—presumably for checking the weight of the hay as it was delivered.

Panmure Place
This street was planned in the 1820s and was to be called Rigg Street after James Home Rigg (see Home St) but was not built until after 1852, when the 2nd Earl of Panmure succeeded to that title and was, at the time, Parliamentary Secretary of War.

Ponton Street
Named after Alexander Ponton, wright and surveyor who owned land in the area and was the architect of a block of houses erected on the west side of the street in 1766. Referred to as Ponton Street at least by 1790 (*Population of St Cuthbert's*).
   His daughter Jean Stewart Ponton was married to Major James Weir, proprietor of the south lands of Tollcross at the turn of the nineteenth century.

Portsburgh Square
Taken from Wester Portsburgh, the small burgh outside the West Port to the old town of Edinburgh (see Chapter 2).

Riego Street
At the turn of the nineteenth century this street was called Tollcross Street. It was renamed Riego Street after the death in 1820 of the proprietor of this part of Tollcross, Major James Weir, who was on active duty in the Royal Marines during the Peninsular Wars.
   The name refers to Don Rafael Riego, Major in the Asturian regiment in

the Spanish Army who in 1820 proclaimed the Constitution of Cadiz. Around this time he visited Britain and came to Edinburgh. He was a well respected democrat of the time who, when King Ferdinand became absolute ruler of Spain, escaped from Cadiz, was captured and brutally executed in 1823.

Sometimes referred to as 'the two Riego Streets' the roadway will be altered to accommodate building developments over 1987–8.

Rosebank Cottages
Erected in 1853 and named after a small area of land in the vicinity (see Chapter 2).

Rosemount Buildings
Erected in 1859 this building is named after the mansion and grounds of Rosemount built in 1785 and owned by William Morrison (see Morrison St).

St David's Place, Terrace
Named after the Church of the same name, the site of which is now occupied by a block of flats built in 1973.

St Peter's Buildings, Place
Named after St Peter's United Free Church, now Viewforth Church.

Semple Street
A brewery to the west corner of Semple and Morrison Streets was bought by John Semple in 1758, who in 1762 was succeeded by Robert Semple. The

Fig 8.6: Semple Street looking north to Morrison Street before the houses were demolished in the 1920s.

street was built at the turn of that century and, until the canal was filled in at this point, there was a wooden bridge over the water.

Previously called Slunk Street, this referred to the muddy and uneven nature of the road.

Spittal Street
Built in 1835 and named after Sir James Spittal, Lord Provost of Edinburgh, between 1833–7.

Tarvit Street
Named after the Fife residence (Tarvit House in Cupar) of James Home Rigg, on whose lands the street was built (see Home St).

Thornybauk
Thornybauk (or Thornybank) means a row of thornbushes, which originally ran from Tollcross to Morrison Street by way of Thornybauk and Semple Street, marking the western border of the lands of Tollcross and the eastern border of Dalry and Wright's Houses. It is likely that it originally formed a continuous line with thorn trees at Drumdryan.

Tobago Street
The houses on this street have now been demolished. Now adjacent to Dewar Place, by the SSEB building, but was originally the name applied to a section of Morrison Street to the east of its present position. Named after Nathaniel Donaldson who lived in Tobago in the West Indies and who sold nearby land to William Morrison (see Morrison St). Nearby there was a Jamaica Street.

Tollcross, West
Built at the turn of the twentieth century and named after the previous street of that name, now part of Home Street.

Tollcross
The pillar clock at Tollcross was gifted to the City of Edinburgh, by Provost Sir James Steel and Treasurer Cranston in 1901 and was one of four similar clocks in the City made by the Edinburgh Clockmakers, James Ritchie & Son. Originally a pendulum clock, in 1926 it became spring driven and was wound once a week by the makers. In 1969 it was converted to electric mechanism. When, in 1974, the crossroads area was being improved to accommodate the widening of Earl Grey Street, the clock was removed and later, after much public pressure, replaced close to its original position.

Torphichen Street, Place
The origin of the name is not clear. Torphichen Street was first called St Cuthbert's Street and was planned to be continued through to Lothian Road. By 1848 these plans were overtaken with the coming of the railway. Torphichen Place was first called Thomas Street, possibly after Thomas Morrison, who owned the land in the 1820s.

Valleyfield Street
Named after the lands of Valleyfield or Villafield, on which the street is built and the mansion of Valleyfield built around 1687.

At one time there was a cattle market and also a market garden ('Marshalls Garden') on this street.

Vennel
Old Scots word, of French origin, for a lane.

Viewforth, Gardens, Square, Terrace
Named after Viewforth House, which occupied the site where Boroughmuir School now stands, because of its view over the River Forth.

West Port
An abbreviation of Wester Portsburgh, the small burgh outwith the Old Town. Also the gate to the Old Town.

Western Approach Road
Denoting an alternative route into the city and offering traffic relief entering the town from the west.

Westhall Gardens
The origin of this name is unclear.

Whitehouse Loan
The section of this street which cuts through Bruntsfield Links was built in 1869 and named after the Mansion of Whitehouse nearby.

Wright's Houses
Named after the Baronial home of William Napier, Wrychtis Houses, south of Gillespie Crescent, and possibly referred to the Laird of Wryte.

Further reading

1 Boog Watson, C B. *Notes, Volumes 1–15*. Manuscript, Edinburgh Room, Central Public Library, Edinburgh.
2 Dunlop, A H, (1890). *Anent Old Edinburgh*.
3 Edinburgh Corporation: City Engineers' Department, (1975). *History and Derivation of Edinburgh Street Names*.
4 Scotland, A W, Taylor, A J, Park, W G, (eds), (1984). *The Streets of Edinburgh*.
5 Smith, John, (c 1920). *Origin, nomenclature and location of various houses, streets and districts in Edinburgh founded during the eighteenth and nineteenth centuries*. Manuscript, Edinburgh Room, Central Public Library, Edinburgh.

9

The Meadows And Links

Jane Curr

Bruntsfield Links

The Links we know today, traversed only by Whitehouse Loan, has retained almost its exact shape since 1586 and is the last unspoilt remnant of the Borough Muir (or moor), reaching out to the Grange and Morningside.

It is not known exactly when the name 'Links' was applied to the land but as late as the end of the seventeenth century it was also known as the Foir or Fore Muir. A record dated 1683 refers to a Merchant, John Marshall, who wanted to build a house on Bruntsfield Links, 'Commonly called Foir Borrow Muir' and this most likely is distinguishing it from the previous name of Burgh Muir.

One of the reasons why the links remained virtually intact after 1586 and was not feued off by the town, as with the rest of the Muir, was the strong influence of the golfing fraternity of Edinburgh. In 1723 the town confirmed:

> The public right of way to play golf, walk on the Links, to dry clothes on the bushes, use springs of water, in the case of infection, the right to erect huts and bury the dead on the Links, the right to muster the City Guard, militia (etc), and to dig quarries, as long as they were filled in after with rubbish.

Again in the Edinburgh Improvement Act 1827 the town forbade the erection of buildings of any kind on the Links (or the Meadows).

The one exception to leisure, domestic and emergency considerations was quarrying for building stone, which seems strange given the growing golfing lobby. However, it was carried out with great consideration to the golfers as can be seen from a record of 1695. The council minutes record:

> Agreed that the tacksman should have liberty to make choice of one acre of any part of the Links for a quarry, where no other person shall get liberty to dig—always at one distance from the place where the neighbours play Goulf.

A succession of quarriers worked the south corner of the Links, evidence of which can still be seen today in the dips and hollows next to Bruntsfield Place. The strict conditions were upheld until the middle of the eighteenth century when the quarrying ceased.

Fig 9.1: Edinburgh Castle from Bruntsfield Links, drawn around 1746. It also shows golf being played and cattle grazing.

Quarries were not the only problem for the golfers and walkers of the eighteenth century. Horses, carts and coaches were a great menace on this open ground, invasion of which, for example, was caused in 1733, when the 'crossbars of entry to the Links' were broken.

By 1797 a frustrated Golf Society was complaining of horse riders 'spoiling the ground for golfers'. They suggested that placards be erected and an advertisement placed in the newspaper to state the problem and appeal for it to cease!

Golf
It is not known when golf was first played on the Links but, as noted, it was certainly known by the end of the seventeenth century. However, the first fully constituted golf club, the Edinburgh Burgess Golfing Society, was not instituted until 1735, followed by the Bruntsfield Links Golf Club in 1761. The Burgess Society met at Bruntsfield until they moved to Musselburgh in 1875.

Golf was obviously a very popular pastime, particularly for the well-to-do, despite the limited golfing season. Those who played had a great influence over the Town Council. In 1791, for example, a plan to build a road on the Links side of Wright's Houses met with great opposition from the Burgess Society. The Road Trustees had intended to bypass the existing road through the village of Wright's Houses, then on the both sides of lower Bruntsfield Place. At that time the road was very narrow and in great disrepair. At the expense of the houses on the west side of the village, which were demolished in 1792, the Town Council declined the request and offered £150 for the upgrading of the existing road.

It is not surprising that Whitehouse Loan was not laid across the Links until 1869, at a time when the population was increasing in the surrounding

Fig 9.2: The old house between the tenements of Barclay Terrace and the modern day Golf Tavern. The photograph is believed to date from around 1930. The house was originally known as Golf Hall and later the Golf House Tavern.

area. It was also prudent of Edinburgh Corporation to lay a first class course on the Braid Hills after its purchase in 1889, responding also to the need for a more extensive course than the Links, which by then must have been frustratingly short given the more advanced clubs and balls being used.

The Golf Tavern

One last area of interest relating to the Links and to golf is the origin of the *Golf Tavern* in Wright's Houses which today boasts above its door that it was established in 1456. Unfortunately there is no evidence available to substantiate this claim but it is possible that by 1711 there had been a Tavern called *Rare Maggy Johnston's* in the area. She died in that year and was remembered in a poem by Allan Ramsay. It was described as being about a mile south of Edinburgh.

At roughly a mile's distance there was a Golf (club) House at Meadow Place, described in a record of 1786, which may have had an early origin as a Tavern. By 1812 Knox's map shows this as 'Old Golf House' and, on the same map, a building at Wright's Houses as simply 'Golf House'.

The latter building was erected in 1716 by James Brownhill, described by James Grant as a 'speculative builder'. In 1760 it was described as:

> A great house of 12 fire rooms, with court, bowling green and garden, enclosed with stone dyke.

It is surprising that this record said nothing of the sale of alcoholic drinks on the premises as it was known that, in 1717, this was the case. However, it is unlikely it was a tavern in the sense we know pubs of today. In fact the house was three storeys high and, if it was not actually built as such, it had, by the mid eighteenth century been converted into separate accommodation. Although it is known that the Bruntsfield Links Club members met in 1787 in the house of Thomas Comb, a clubmaker, he is known to have lived on the first floor only and was certainly not a publican.

The house was known primarily as Golf Hall until the beginning of the nineteenth century, although for a while it was also referred to as Foxton. The change of the name to Golf House in the 1820s suggests that it was a Golf Club House (at least in part) and it is likely that the club house was also a tavern.

The position of Golf Hall in Wright's Houses was adjacent to modern day Barclay Terrace and can be seen clearly on the 1852 Ordnance Survey map. By that date it is referred to as the *Golf House Tavern* and it was still there in 1887. Photographic evidence suggests that it survived well into the twentieth century.

The Golf Tavern building that we know today is of early nineteenth century origin and was a private residence until late that century. It is not known when it was converted into a tavern but it is known for certain that it was given its red sandstone exterior and its interior design in 1899. However, in spite of the late birth of a tavern to the present site, it can still claim to be the successor of a number of establishments in the vicinity which catered for the golfer.

Sadly there are few who now play on the Links and fewer still who, after a game, would gravitate to the pub to discuss the day's golf.

The Meadows

Today the Meadows serves as a source of recreation and leisure for the people of Edinburgh. However, through the ages the Meadows has played a variety of roles; industrial, as a water supply, agricultural and more recently as a public park. During this time there have been conflicts of interest between the use of the Meadows by the city and for individual purposes.

Originally a loch covered the entire area now occupied by the Meadows. Bordering on the Borough Muir, the King's parklands, it was called the Burgh Loch. However, in the fifteenth century the North Loch was formed where Princes Street Gardens now lie, and the Burgh Loch became known as the South Loch.

In the sixteenth century the loch's primary purpose was as a water supply for the city. Various Acts were passed to conserve it. At the head of the loch, at the west end, the water drained off by a small stream—the run of the loch—hence the name Lochrin, still used today. A dyke was also constructed there to keep the water in.

In 1568 a John Lawson of High Riggs complained that the dyke was preventing the irrigation of his lands. He took matters into his own hands and during the night pulled down the dyke so as his lands were flooded with water. The magistrates therefore ordered 'All the inhabitants of the burgh, merchants, craftsmen and all the uthirs without exceptioun' each with 'schole and mattock and spaid' to repair the damage. It is not known what punishment Lawson endured but during that time a number of people were imprisoned for breaching the dyke.

This was a time of drought and plague and in 1575 the brewers were instructed to fetch their water directly from the South Loch rather than the city wells due to water shortage in the city.

In 1597-8 the loch was conveyed to the newly formed Fellowship and Society of Ale and Beer Brewers of the Burgh of Edinburgh. The contract included a provision forbidding the Society to alter the run of the water from the Loch to conserve it for the use of the citizens. The Society had to pay an annual duty of twenty merks for the use of the loch but this period of almost exclusive use by the brewers was comparatively short-lived. In 1617 there were problems with the payment of the duty and in 1618 the society was dissolved and the loch restored to the magistrates.

The intensive use had, however, left its mark and by 1619, 'the loch had become considerably reduced in size and area and its waters muddy. So much so that the Magistrates instructed that the run of the Loch be closed. It was at this time that the name of the 'Meadows' developed. The water had receded to such an extent that the surrounding area was being used to graze animals.

At this time plans were drawn up to bring water from the springs at Comiston although it was not until 1672 that the pipes were actually laid.

From Loch to Park

The endeavours of the brewers had inadvertently hastened the process of draining the loch although it was over two centuries later before the draining process was finally completed.

In 1657 the council agreed to drain the loch. The Town Council minutes report that the loch was drained by English soldiers and then finished by 'five poor Scotsmen'.

The following year the Meadows and the Links were feued to John Straiton, merchant burgess, for a tack duty of £1000 Scots along with the fishing rights. His period of tenure was doomed to financial failure and he was only partly successful in his endeavours. During the 1660s the Magistrates were inundated with a string of complaints from Straiton. 'Invasion by horse and bestial for watering so that he cannot be able to pay his rent.'

By 1678 he was imprisoned in the Tolbooth for non-payment of rent. However, he was released on petition by his wife, 'to maw the grass and dig the stanks thereof' on the understanding his son-in-law put up the bail. However, this was by no means the end of Straiton's problems. In the 1680s, being unable to put up the money to keep himself out of jail, Straiton resigned the lease of the Burgh Loch. The town agreed to give him a pension of 500 merks but this was reduced to 300 merks per year as the town subtracted the outstanding rent.

William Carfrae and five others took over the lease in 1695 for a period of twenty-seven years, and during this time they agreed to construct a walk and a ditch around the whole loch and to plant ash, elm or fig trees. However, it was not until 1722 that the Meadows began to resemble the present layout when Thomas Hope of Rankeillor took over a fifty-seven year lease.

Hope was a landowner in Fife, an advocate and for a time a member of Parliament. Initially he had wanted the public to be excluded from the Meadows for the first seven years of his tenure while the drainage work went on. However, popular demand for this amenity was so great that he was forced to change his mind. The walkway round the Meadows was retained as well as a tree-lined avenue, with ditches on either side, across the Meadows.

Access to the Meadows from the Town had always been a problem. However, in 1737, an extension to the Meadow Walk was laid, taking it up to Lauriston. Part of George Heriot's land was feued and a roadway was constructed (in the position of modern day Forrest Road) providing access to Candlemaker Row and, thereby the Town through the old Flodden Wall.

A summer house, the Cage, was constructed at the southern end of Middle Meadow Walk but it was removed in the 1820s. By this time the lead on the top of the roof had been removed in frequent instances of vandalism. At this time the Meadows were also known as Hope Park. Streets bearing the name of Thomas Hope can be found to the East of the Meadows.

Unfortunately Thomas Hope suffered great financial hardship as a consequence of his work on the Meadows. He died in 1771, in a house at the east end of the former loch without being paid a penny.

By this time the drainage of the Meadows was by no means complete. Even as late as 1806 there were problems with stagnant water. The situation was further complicated by sewage from the surrounding houses. Legislation of 1785 and 1787 conferred power to construct a drain from the east of the Meadows to the King's Park which was enacted in 1804:

> To carry off the filth and ordure which the common sewers . . . discharge into the open casts . . . and which have been allowed to stagnate there, to the great danger of the health of the inhabitants and total annihilation of their necessary exercise and recreation in the place intended for general resort.

However, James Haig, the owner of Lochrin Distillery (see Chapter 3), objected to this alleging that the drain to the east would draw away the water he used for 'cooling his worms', (i.e. the condensation pipes). The case lasted from 1806 to 1812 finally being resolved with the two parties coming to a compro-

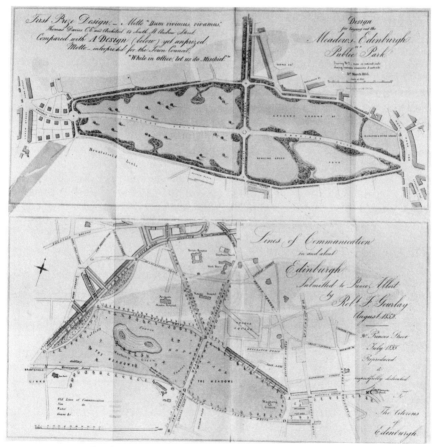

Fig 9.3: Designs for the layout of the Meadows put forward in 1855 by Thomas Davies and Robert Gourlay which, like many, were not used.

mise. The magistrates could draw of the foul water while Haig was entitled to the 'spring or other water flowing into or rising in the meadows, and rain water.'

During the nineteenth century the plans to drain the Meadows from the east finally went ahead and drainage of the Meadows was at last completed. This happened when the Police Commissioners held the lease of the Meadows. Under the contract the Commissioners were obliged to improve the drainage of the Meadows.

Layout

In 1854 an article appeared in *The Scotsman*. It criticised the lack of public access to the Meadows with only one entrance at Forrest Road and railings all the way round. 'It appears to us that the Meadows have never been sufficiently appreciated by the citizens . . . as a public park fairly considered.' They proposed a carriageway and an entrance at the North West corner of the Meadows.

A competition for suggestions for the new layout of the Meadows was run in 1855. The winner was Thomas Davies whose plan included a carriageway running right through the middle of the Meadows from east to west. His design was criticised by Robert Gourlay who drew up an alternative. Charles McIntosh was commissioned by the Commissioners of Police to draw up a plan for the layout of the Meadows. Although McIntosh's plans were not completely accepted, they influenced the layout of the Meadows we know today.

As a result of these plans Melville Drive was laid and was officially opened on 25 January 1859. It was named after the Lord Provost of that time, Sir John Melville.

The Function of the Meadows

Agriculture

After draining, the green open spaces of the Meadows were exploited to the full in a variety of ways. Cattle, horses and sheep were grazed there and, in the case of sheep, well into the twentieth century. Thomas Hope of Rankeillor helped in the formation of a Society for the Improvement of the Knowledge of Agriculture. They met locally and carried out experiments in the nearby Meadows. In a report of 1914 the different methods of keeping the grass cut are described. The West Meadows were mowed and the East Meadows were grazed by sheep!

Agriculture returned to the Meadows during the Second World War. The war changed the face of the Meadows for its duration. The west side of the meadows was cultivated as part of the 'Digging for Victory' campaign. The ground was given over to the people to plant vegetables as part of the war effort. In 1860 the Council had accepted proposals for forming further walkways, a bowling green and erecting a band stand. Sadly the bandstand was removed in 1953 after it had fallen into disrepair during the war. As well as the allotments part of the Meadows was used as an emergency landing ground for helicopters servicing the Royal Infirmary and the Sick Children's Hospital. Air raid shelters were built alongside Melville Drive.

Recreation

The Meadows has also been used for recreational purposes down the years. One of the longest established sports was archery practised there by the Royal Company of Archers. The Company was constituted in 1676 having originated earlier that century with a body of noblemen and gentlemen who met for the encouragement of archery. In 1776 the building of Archers' Hall commenced in a site on the side of the Meadows, at the corner of Buccleuch Street and Meadow Lane. Various additions and modifications were added over the years and in 1889 the building was completely rebuilt.

In 1822 the Company offered their services as a bodyguard to the George IV on his visit to Edinburgh that year. The services were accepted and since then the Archers have furnished a body guard for the Sovereign whenever he or she is in residence in Holyrood Palace. Today the Archers have moved their practice and competition grounds to Holyrood although they parade annually in the Meadows.

Thomas Hope of Rankeillor offered the Archers a piece of ground in the East meadows in 1726 during the period of his lease. It is recorded that:

> The Royal Company therefore were now enabled for the first time not only to enjoy butt-shooting in permanent and agreeable surroundings, but to adjourn to their own Hall for subsequent refreshment, instead of having to resort to a tavern.

Among the many notable people who have 'shot their arrows' in the Meadows was Charles X of France who was living in Holyrood Palace during his exile. On a lighter note it is reported that old men sitting on the stone benches watching the archers did not hold the skills of the King's Body Guard in very high regard. 'I think if I was Peter I would aye stand richt in front of the target: a body would be safer there!'

Archery is the longest established sport connected with the Meadows but by no means the only one. The Edinburgh Bowling Club was founded in 1848 and reputedly plays on the oldest ground in the city, adjacent to the old Archery ground at the east end of the Meadows. The East Meadows was the birth place of Association Football. Edinburgh's present day 'Big Clubs', the Heart of Midlothian and Hibernian began in the Meadows but the game became so popular that the private grounds of Tynecastle and Easter Road were built. Nowadays amateur clubs use the Meadows for weekend football.

Another established sport on the Meadows is cricket. Although a typically English sport, cricket has been played there since early last century. In 1834 the Town Council granted permission for the leaseholder at that time to let a portion of the Meadows to the Brunswick Cricket Club. However, in 1848 a petition for a student cricket ground there was turned down.

Eight ash tennis courts were built in 1914 in the East Meadows. Such was their popularity that they have been extended and there are now sixteen.

Open air draughts also took place at the east end of the Meadows. This novel construction, made from tiles which the corporation had no further use for, was the first of its kind in Scotland, and was opened on 12 May 1933. At the turn of the century another popular game was quoits.

A more unusual use of the Meadows was proposed in 1842. Plans had been put forward to build a racecourse in the Meadows but obviously such a specialised activity was outweighed by the interests of the general public and the Town Council turned down the idea.

Nowadays the Meadows is used for early morning and late evening joggers who tread the paths of the Meadows as part of the growing health consciousness of the 1980s.

Public Speaking

Public speaking on religious and political topics was very popular in the East Meadows at the turn of the century. So much so that it shared the title of 'Edinburgh's Forum' with the Mound. William Anderson, a coalman with St Cuthbert's Cooperative, who lived in Tollcross, described in his journal such a meeting in 1905. He was a Socialist and sympathised with the Social Democratic Federation led by John McLean. McLean was visiting Edinburgh that summer and attempted to speak on the Meadows:

> What a din was in the Meadows, caused by the unearthly blasting of a Hallelujah Band. They broke the elements and all the meetings were postponed. McLean's mind was confused with the din. He told me he could hear ever so many bands playing and ever so many men talking.

The above activities were subject to the often strict byelaws of the parks. Playing of games was prohibited on Sundays until quite recently, although special concessions were granted. In most of Edinburgh's public parks public gatherings were prohibited. However, the Meadows were one of the few places where this was allowed.

Cycling

> Hitherto it has been a quiet shady retreat. Under the wide spreading branches of the trees of that Avenue, old citizens, sick and infirm citizens, blind citizens, nursery maids with children, have found a shelter, free from the casualties which are likely to occur in a public street.

This appeared in a newspaper in 1873 after rumours that the council was going to cut down the trees on Middle Meadow Walk and open it up to carriages. Through public pressure the council relented and it was over a hundred years later that wheeled vehicles, in the form of bicycles, were allowed down Middle Meadow Walk.

The concession was granted after pressure by the cyclist campaigning body, *Spokes*. In the past few years a special cycle team has been formed on the Regional council to represent better the needs of the growing number of cyclists. North Meadow walk is now a cycle path and there are plans to open up the other Meadows Walks to cyclists to try and regulate the illegal cycling. In 1988 a cycle crossing was opened at the southern end of Middle Meadow Walk, across Melville Drive.

As with the nineteenth century issue about carriages, there has been a strong campaign against cycling on the Meadows led by a Tollcross pensioner who fears for the safety of pedestrians on the Walks and would like to see cycling there banned completely. In the early 1980s he compiled a petition of names, including headteachers and church ministers, who have lodged their opposition to cycling. A heated debate has taken place in the pages of the *Evening News*. For the moment, however, it seems as if the objectors have lost the argument and pedestrians and cyclists will have to coexist together on the Meadows for some time to come.

Exhibitions and Festivals
The open spaces of the Meadows have been used to host a variety of large scale public events, the most notable being in 1886 when the International Exhibition of Industry, Science and Art was held there. The exhibition was on a grand scale rivalling that of the London and Paris exhibitions of previous years. The buildings erected for the purpose covered most of the West Meadows.

The exhibition was opened by Prince Albert Victor on 6 May 1886. The Royal procession travelled down the Mound, along Princes Street and up

Fig 9.4: A photograph of the buildings occupied by the 1886 Exhibition of Industry, Art and Science held on the West Meadows. The model dwelling house designed by James Gowans can be seen in the foreground.

Lothian Road to the entrance of the exhibition at the end of Brougham Place. The streets were crowded with people and decorated for the occasion. The scene was described in *The Scotsman* the following day:

> On the facades, shields of elegant designs were backed by flags and other trophies, and balconies were draped with coloured cloth embroidered with natural and artificial flowers, while flags waved from house tops and hung from windows.

Parallels can be drawn with the Great Exhibition of 1851 in London although the Edinburgh exhibition went one better. It was able to stay open after dark due to the installation of electric lamps (3200 in total) powered by nine dynamos!

The plans for the event were conceived in 1884 when it was felt that the Scottish economy needed a boost. After the plans were laid before the Town Council it took a few months before they could be persuaded as to the financial viability of the venture.

The complex of Exhibition Halls, thirty-four in all, was housed under a substantial brick building with iron and glass domes. The insecure Meadows soil made it necessary to sink twelve feet deep piles into the ground to support the structure which was designed by architects J Burnett and Son. The exhibition hall was 1000 feet long and 300 feet wide. It consisted of two parts; a grand pavillion at the west end continued into a 970 feet long range of courts on either side of a central corridor at the east end.

The 1886 exhibition was a showcase for the latest scientific and industrial

Fig 9.5: Artefacts from the 1886 Exhibition of Industry, Art and Science held on the Meadows now in the safe-keeping of the Huntly House Museum.

developments of the day. Transport and heavy industry were exhibited and the latest domestic gadgets were on view in a model cottage designed by the architect James Gowan. It had two stories and was built for two working class families. In conjunction with the more practical exhibits the arts were represented in fine art, sculpture and photography. There was also a special section with embroidery and needlework for women.

James Gowan, who designed the model dwelling house, played a large part in the organisation of the exhibition. He was a son of a mason and trained as an architect. It is thought he lived in Rosebank Cottages for four years. He was chairman of the Executive Council of the Merchant Society, under whose auspices the exhibition took place. Stone from his quarries was used in some of the exhibitions and to construct parts of the building. He was knighted when Queen Victoria visited the exhibition.

The massive construction was dismantled in October 1886. The total cost had been £40 000 and, during the six months, it had been visited by two and a half million people. At the end, the exhibition registered a £20 000 profit. It had indeed been a financial success as well as a promotional success for Edinburgh and Scotland.

Today reminders of the exhibition can still be found in the Meadows. The commemorative pillars, designed by James Gowan, stand at the east and west ends. At the west end too stands the Prince Albert sundial. Jawbone Walk takes its name from the whale jawbone arch at the Melville Drive end of the walk.

In more recent times the Meadows has been used for a different kind of festival. In 1975 the first Meadows Neighbourhood Festival was held. It aimed to involve community groups and local residents in a festival of arts, entertainment and sport. In his introduction in the 1975 Festival programme, Bailie George Foulkes said:

> The first ever Meadows Festival is an attempt by local residents and others active in various committees around the Meadows, to provide an opportunity for us all to enjoy ourselves.

The festival is still organised by a group of volunteers from the surrounding communities. Because it is held in the open air the weather plays a large part in the success of the event and although held in June it has often suffered from torrential rain! The festival is financed from stall charges and grants from the local council. If a profit is made it has been a tradition to share it out among needy community groups.

In 1981 the Meadows Festival was in crisis. They had £1000 in debts. Lucie Mackenzie, secretary at the time, said in the *Evening News*, 'If we don't get solvent again and get more support from local people to run the Festival then it may have to finish.' Happily, though, support and funding were forthcoming and the Festival is alive and well today.

Further reading

1 Bruce, William Moir, (1918). *The Burgh Muir of Edinburgh*. BOEC, **10**.
2 Boog Watson, C B. *Notes, Volumes 1–15*. Manuscript, Edinburgh Room, Central Public Library, Edinburgh.
3 Edinburgh District Council, City of: Libraries Division, (1986). *No Ordinary Man: The Journal of William Anderson 1902–06*.
4 Cameron, J A, (1886). *Guide to the International Exhibition*.
5 Cant, Malcolm, (1984). *Marchmont in Edinburgh*.
6 Hay, Iain, (1951). *The Royal Company of Archers 1676–1951*.
7 Kemp, Edward, (1873). *Report and plan for laying out and planting the Meadows*.
8 Maitland, W, (1753). *A History of Edinburgh from its foundation to the present time*.

10

Tollcross and Fountainbridge Remembered

Drew Easton

Introduction

Looking at Tollcross and district today it is not easy to imagine that, in the first half of this century, it was a much more densely populated area, with remarkable contrasts between the different communities, especially in terms of housing and social class. Today, what remains of a once thriving community seems busy enough; Home Street, Leven Street, Bread Street, Brougham Place, Lothian Road, Lauriston Place and Morrison Street remain largely intact. However, as many other streets were not as fortunate and gone are the shops, the industry and, more importantly, the people, many of whom moved to the outskirts of the City in the period between 1950 and 1970. The West Port, High Riggs, Ponton Street, Riego Street, Earl Grey Street, Brandfield Street, Freer Street, Newport Street and, most important of all, Fountainbridge, have all suffered from an enforced exodus which, even in 1988, has not yet been reversed, except in very small measure.

The area around Fountainbridge was considered by its residents as a community in itself. Tollcross was 'posh' by comparison. It included the top half of Grove Street, Upper Grove Place, Brandfield Street (now only two stairs remaining), Freer Street (opposite Grove Street but now gone without trace) and Chalmers Buildings. As can be seen in the table below, in 1920, the street Fountainbridge had no less than 387 households, 105 shops, 17 offices and 5 public houses. In addition there were 17 other establishments including three stables, four warehouses, a rubber mill, a brewery, a toy factory, a 'rag and bone' merchants, a bakery, two picture houses and two schools.

A similar picture can be seen of the West Port and the High Riggs which can be compared to what now exists in the 1980s. Although the West Port is slowly being returned to its former position as a distinct community it may never compare to its earlier years. As a consequence of redevelopment of the so-called 'SMT triangle' the High Riggs, once a main route from the south to the Old Town, will soon cease to exist as a road when it has been completed.

	Houses	Shops	Offices	Public Houses
Lothian Road	109	61	10	4
Home Street	155	47	5	1
Fountainbridge	387	105	17	5
High Riggs	116	16	1	2
West Port	294	62	3	4

(*Source*: Valuation Rolls, 1920–1).

Talking to people today about life in Tollcross prior to 1960, one gets a strong sense of these different communities in the area, which in some cases were single streets (e.g. Glen Street). One did not have to walk far to work, to shop or to enjoy the local entertainments. Schools were on your doorstep, Churches round the corner and whatever you could not buy in one shop you would get up the street. Princes Street and the Bridges were for special occasions. Perhaps a Saturday afternoon treat would be to visit Patrick Thomson's for tea and cakes or, if it was warm, to sit in Princes Street Gardens or dance to bands playing at the Ross Bandstand. Life for most people was parochial in nature and one could not often (if ever) afford to shop in Princes Street or compete for jobs in other parts of the town. Even when one was out of work the local Labour Exchange at Riego Street was never more than a few streets away.

To younger people this description of the area might sound claustrophobic but to anyone brought up in the city centre during this period it was a fine place to be. Individuals remember it as it was with affection and enthusiasm. Indeed some people who left the area in the 1950s and 1960s still hold reunions on a regular basis, such is the bond they feel to one another and the community which was lost.

Fig 10.1: Some members of the Fountainbridge Reminiscence Society in 1988. They meet four times a year in Slateford.

Childhood Memories

In the days before television, much of a child's entertainment was self generated, apart from visits to the cinema or listening to the radio. Children's Hour, Monday Night at Eight, the Tommy Hanley Show and Life with the Lyons were particular radio favourites. The cinema was fairly cheap and was a very popular social occasion. For example the Poole's Synod Hall in Castle Terrace (as differentiated from the Poole's Roxy in Gorgie) was more than just a place to see films:

> They used to run the Mickey Mouse Club. Most of the kids were in it and when it came to your birthday you used to get a nice birthday card from them. And you also used to be able to get into the cinema for nothing and take a friend with you on your birthday. And you got a bar of chocolate and you had your badge with Mickey Mouse on it.

> Our Saturday afternoons were often spent at the matinees of the Coliseum Cinema in Fountainbridge—threepence admission. This was more expensive than some. The Blue Hall in Lauriston Street was cheaper and the Tollcross in Lauriston Place was a penny.

> I can remember meeting my younger brother who told me he couldn't stop—he was going to see Tom Mix, the cowboy hero of the day. I didn't think there was a Tom Mix film on but I have since read that he did make a personal visit to the Coliseum, and hence the big hurry!

School also played a big part in a child's life as can be seen from memories of the war years when all the male teachers were called up and the school was sometimes used by the Forces.

> There wasn't so many teachers left and then they farmed us out to houses. People in the area, you know, let out rooms and you went to that person's house to get your schooling. There were two houses in Morrison Street . . . one half way down and (the other) just at the top opposite the cinema. I don't know what they got paid for it. Maybe about ten of you might go . . . for a couple of hours. It was every day you used to go. It was different from going to the classroom, going to someone's house!

Other memories of working out of school which had a clear impact on an older pupil at Darroch off Gilmore Place describes a girl's education in a house at Leamington Terrace owned by the School and at a local nursery:

> You got to do all the different chores. You used to get to wash the clothes in that little blue dye, dolly dye. And then you got ironing, you got taught to clean the step wi' the white clay and then you used to get cooking. Then you used to get taught how to serve, lay the table and setting it. They had the linen napkins in the rings.

> There was a nursery in St Peter's Place which . . . you used to go there and bath the babies. You practised on a doll when you first went . . . and then you actually got to go and work with the children. They were getting us ready for marriage. That was the basic thing, you know, that you wouldn't work once you'd got married, you'd just 'thingmy' the home and have children!

Like children of all generations the Tollcross child looked forward to buying sweets. Fountainbridge dwellers will remember McKay's Sweetie Shop where you could buy 'the most mouth-watering toffee doddles' which one person described as a sweet which 'would make any modern dentist really cringe'. Another shop on Fountainbridge was an Ice Cream and Confectionery owned by a well known man in Fountainbridge called Tammy Lang:

> He was reputed to have the loudest voice at Tynecastle, as it was said his voice could be heard well above the rest when cheering on the Hearts!

For the less well off (or for the opportunist) you could sometimes get from the Brewers Food Supplies a piece of what was known locally as Locus, which was very sweet and had a hard covering. A local person discovered in later years this was a delicacy for the brewery horses.

In a dairy next to the chip shop on the corner of Drumdryan Street you could buy Vantas:

> It was just coloured water but, oh, we used to go daft over it. We used to come through from Glen Street where we were playing and you got it in a glass. It was a halfpenny. I suppose it was the forerunner to lemonade. Vimto was another thing you got there.

During this period the number of sweetie shops in the area was staggering. Many more will be remembered but the reader will certainly get 'the flavour' of both the shops and the sweets from memories such as these:

> When I was wee you used to go to Casey's Sweetshop in Lauriston Place and you used to get a lucky potato. Sometimes you got a halfpenny in it. It was brown stuff, like powdered chocolate, with an unusual sort of taste, sort of chewy inside. Then the macaroon bars—if you got a pink one you got another one free. They were mostly white. Then there was sweetie cigarettes, liquorice and lucky bags. And M and M's in Earl Grey Street (there) they used to take all the odds and ends of all the range of chocolates—they had jars and jars—and when it got to the end (of the jars) they would pop them in a sixpenny bag assortment.

Glen Street was a popular place for children, not least because it had two schools facing one another, Catholic and Episcopal. It was also fairly secluded and, although there was not a great deal of traffic around during this period, trams coming up and down Lauriston Place would have been a great danger. Despite this, football playing in the street was frowned upon. Indeed one former player remembers:

> You used to play football until the Polis came, then you'd run away . . . through the lane to Panmure Place, then all spread out! You were really master criminals playing football. It just showed you the crime the police had to contend with when they made such a big deal out of playing football!

And yet fond memories of building bonfires for Guy Fawkes and Victoria Day at the end of Glen Street suggest that safety and crime were a contradiction! However, such celebrations were not without 'criminal' intent:

> You used to have battles because you'd be away collecting stuff for the bonfire, you'd maybe leave two or three on guard and then a gang would come from another street and run off with so much . . . and then you'd go and take it back!

Fig 10.2: The children of Glen Street in 1923.

On a more constructive level back green and street concerts in Glen Street and Drumdryan Street in particular, were very popular, especially in the War years:

> I remember back green concerts. The mothers made costumes out of crepe paper, skirts and capes. It was to raise money for the Soldiers, Sailors and Airmen Fund, and it was fun for the kids, they did something—sung and danced—and then you collected money. The younger kids would do that and the mothers would all come and stand and pay something for watching.

Concerts were also held in the All Saints' Church and in the Episcopal School which were particularly keen to attend to the welfare of children. The school was very popular after classes:

> We used to love it. It was sort of spooky. We went up on our own. None of us went to that School but the Minister at the time was very good. You'd pop round and have a word with him and he'd give you the keys and let you go as long as you left everything the way you got it.

Although there is some evidence of friction between pupils in the two Glen Street Schools, children mixed well in play and tended to treat denominational activities with equality:

> When we were kids we went to all the Sunday Schools. We used to go to the Gospel Hall, in Lauriston Place. we used to go to the Salvation Army, we used to go to the Catholic Church, we used to go to our own Church. I don't know why but we just used to because we played wi' kids that were—you know—nobody bothered about religion. You played wi' Catholic children, Salvation Army children, children that went to the Gospel Hall and that.

The Sunday School in the Freer Street Mission of St Cuthberts Church was more popular with non-local children however, an account given by a former resident of Tollcross tells the sad tale of when as a boy and his friends never reached the Sunday School with the money for the collection plate—it had been taken off them by local lads almost as soon as they had turned into Freer Street.

Sunday Schools also organised picnics to Balerno and Juniper Green, Davidson's Mains and Colinton Dell:

> and of course you always had a new pair of white rubbers . . . like the sort of sneaker things they have nowadays . . . like a gym shoe. And you'd have a nice new dress and you used to have a tinnie, a tin cup on a piece of tape and you used to have that round you! Oh, it was great! You got all your games and races and that sort of thing, and then you got your hot pies and ice puddings. It was great!

The summer also brought the 'Shows' to Lochrin and Fountainbridge:

> I remember Codona's Shows which were held at the Fountainbridge end of Gardner's Crescent. My most vivid memory of the Shows was the Cake Walk. This was a sort of wooden bridge which shunted back and forward making it very difficult to reach the other side.
>
> There was also a Boxing Booth which stayed on after the Shows had gone. Appearing there was Edinburgh's well known boxer Tansy Lee—Professional Boxer.

Those lucky enough to get away for a holiday might have taken a Church organised trip to Humbie Children's Village—not always very popular—or perhaps down the coast to Port Seton or across the Forth by ferry to Burntisland from Granton.

Shopping

As seen in the introduction, Tollcross and district was a busy shopping area for a large population. Small shops were prolific; supermarkets were unheard of:

> Supermarkets killed the small shops. You'd never have visualised a Supermarket. I used to go the messages on a Saturday morning when I was younger and I'd go to Brannen's the butchers, then Murrays the baker, then, to the Pork Butcher in Home Street. Then there was Low's the grocers then Drummonds the fruit shop. Then Grubers the Pork Butcher—we used to go there for black pudding and what they call red sausage. I had a list. We always went to the Store for the plain bread (in those days it wasn't sliced and was wrapped in tissue paper).
>
> The shops were mostly all family businesses.
>
> Tollcross was a super shopping centre and busy. Earl Grey Street on a Saturday afternoon you could hardly move. And the same with Home Street; it was mobbed. And Lauriston Place.

There was very often two or three shops in the one street selling the same produce. Each had its particular clientele and even then, especially with the butchers, there were often queues on a Saturday.

Fig 10.3: Earl Grey Street looking north, showing the busy shops in 1914.

A shop my mother liked to go to was Smiths (in Fountainbridge); she liked the lady who served there. She must have felt quite strongly about this because we passed quite a few good grocers shops on the way, including Pearks two or three doors down. Smiths had a very good and pleasant assistant and they sold fish and sundries. The other half sold groceries with not much room in the middle for customers.

Earl Grey Street was a very popular shopping street, only one side of which remains, the other demolished in the late 1960s. People remember with some sadness the demise of M & M's, Lipton's, Barnett's, Waddel's, Lawrie's, Bennet's, Maitland Radio, Rankin's, Saltman's, Stead and Simpson's and Carr's on the one side and the closure of Blyth's and Fleming's stores on the other.

St Cuthbert's 'Store' (now Scotmid) too was popular, not least because it offered a reasonable dividend on goods bought.

That was . . . a great event, twice a year, the Store dividend. It used to be worth something then. It was a great, great event 'cause you used to go twice a year and get the dividend and your mother would be able to buy things. All the neighbours would be there. The mothers all used to go and the kids would be there, you would meet people. There was always queues. It was quite a good amount of money at the time. It used to be so much in the pound, depending on what year it was and how much you'd spent. Everybody had a store number and you had to go according to what your number was.

Apart from groceries and general household goods the Store had a laundry service, a funeral service and function rooms for weddings and so on. The nearest function suite was the Clifton Rooms in Keir Street off Lauriston Place.

The Store had everything. Employees of the Store (who had children), any children used to get to go to the Christmas Parties. They were held at what they called Port Hamilton at the corner of Gardner's Crescent. They were good (and) it was all free.

The Store dropped off with the competition. And then, of course, once the likes of Marks & Spencers came in to Edinburgh and British Home Stores (and) Littlewoods . . . then people had more money so they weren't relying on the Co-op. Plus the Store didn't really move with the times. You know their goods were old fashioned and people wanted something more modern. Certainly they're trying to catch up now.

Even as this chapter is being written one can hear the demolition of part of the Store complex at Fountainbridge where the Port Hamilton Bakery, Milk Depot and Transport Department was housed. The site has been sold to private developers.

The War Years

Before and during the war food was not packaged in the way it is now.

When you went to the Co-op they had big drawers and all the stuff would be in there: custard powder, rice, sugar, semolina, sago and tea; they used to use a scoop and put it in brown bags, with a special way of folding the top.

Rationing was a big feature during the war years when food was in short supply.

Two ounces of butter was the ration during the War. You couldn't get eggs. It was just powdered egg, except for an egg a week on ration. There was a problem with food for the hens. But there were a lot of people who came round for food for the pigs, to collect the pig swill—potato peelings and so on.

My mother used to make omelettes from dried eggs. Some people didn't seem to like using dried eggs but she seemed to manage to do that. But very occasionally maybe a soldier or somebody would come, having visited a friend, and actually brought a real shell egg and you took it and fried it carefully and took it back on a plate and everyone else would sit looking . . . an EGG!

During the war not only was food in short supply, unfortunately nearly all the Ice Cream Shops and Chip Shops in the area closed down:

There were no fish and chip shops till after the War because they were run by Italians. They were all interned on the Isle of Man. And a lot of the Ice Cream shops went too because they were Italian owned. I suppose they (the Government) felt they had to do that. They couldn't take a chance in case of sabotage or something. It caused a lot of ill feeling against the British. People were quite bitter about being interned because they thought themselves as British. It ruined a lot of their lives.

Many of the families of Italian origin still trade in Edinburgh and some in the Tollcross area. In the 1920s names such as Franceso Crolla, Biagio Boni, John Brattisani and John, Frank and Giovanni Appolinari will be remembered. We still have some of the best fish and chip shops and ice cream parlours in Scotland thanks to Italian immigrants at the turn of the century.

Before Betting Shops were made legal in 1960 there were a number of 'Bookies' in the area, particularly in Freer Street and the High Riggs.

Fig 10.4: Food packaging before the war was completely different from today. This shop in Morrison Street shows milk sold in churns in 1925.

The Bookie used to stand up the lane (Belfrage Lane off the High Riggs). Jimmy Lugton was his name. It was all illegal. It was silly because the Police used to come and pick him up. They would tell him. The boy would hand all his lines to his mate and his mate would go away with them. It was all acceptable that they (the Police) would come down and do High Riggs in July and St Leonards in October and it went like that. But it was really silly. Come 6.00 pm he'd be back to pay out. He could dispose of the winnings in ten minutes. He had to be in the same place. It was known to everybody that the Bookie was standing there. Occasionally they decided to pick him up. He'd write out a slip to himself and this is what was produced in Court. All the punters had nomdeplumes, for example 'The Milkman', to identify you. The names were often as comical as the names of the racehorses.

As rationing became more stringent, Edinburgh Corporation, in 1941, opened up its first British Restaurant situated in West Fountainbridge School. One of eighteen in Edinburgh it was open to all age groups providing cheap and nourishing food. It was called the 'Naebours Tryst' and was visited by the King and Queen in that year. The following year saw the opening of another restaurant, the St Thomas, in the Church of the same name, next to the Rutland Hotel at the West End. The St Thomas was one of two restaurants that stayed open until 1953.

Luckily plans to quickly expand these facilities in the event of destructive war raids were never acted upon. Edinburgh escaped large scale bombing and the nearest bomb dropped on the South Side was in Marchmont in 1940. Not surprising therefore that people became blasée about air raids.

> There was a shelter across from us but there was a three storey tenement above it. It was down in the basement so what would have happened if the tenement was struck, you would've never have got out. My mum and dad would never leave the house 'cause my dad used to sleep through the raids. He said "If I'm gonna be bombed, I'll be bombed" and he would never move. My mother wouldn't leave him so my brother used to take me and pop me in the shelter. Then him and his pals used to roam the streets.
>
> There'd be all ma pals, probably, and their mothers and fathers. You just got used to it. We never really knew anything about the war because the only time that I can vaguely remember any bombs, they bombed a bond in Duff Street, off Dalry. I remember mother taking me to see the shell of the thing. But I mean we were fortunate we never really were frightened that we'd get bombed or anything.
>
> There was a shelter actually in the street. An upright one. But nobody ever used them. It was a brick one . . . at the end of Glen Street. But nobody ever used it. we used to play in it when we were kids.

The 'blackout' is recalled in an amusing account:

> You got used to the blackout. There was one night ma mother and I were coming back from the Oddfellows hall and we were just passing Heriot's School and this man was coming along and he had a big white handkerchief on his front and he kept shouting all the time 'Don't bump into me, don't bump into me! I mean you couldn't possibly bump into him cause you could see him coming!
>
> You were only allowed a torch pointing down the way and that had to be sorta blacked out. Then again you probably didn't go out in the blackout. The trams stopped running when an air raid came on and the rest of the time the lights would be covered somehow.

Industry

Up to the 1950s Fountainbridge was the hub of industry in the area around Tollcross. For those who lived nearby the memories of a sight, sound and smell are vivid.

> The Brewery and the Rubber Mill were two huge places in Fountainbridge. And when they all came out at the same time, you just couldn't see Fountainbridge

for people. The horns used to go at 7 o'clock and 8 o'clock and the lunch break. The brewery whistle and the mill horns let the staff know at five minutes to seven—it was time to start work. Then again let them know when to finish—at five o'clock.

There was always a smell of beer and rubber, and McKays Sweetie factory. You used to be able to tell what kind of boilings they were making that day because of the smell. McKays Toffee is still going around.

The 'Brewery Clock', as it was known, kept everyone with the correct time, especially as clocks were not quite so reliable then. It was also handy for timing the buses which ran from Ardmillan to Easter Road.

The Brewery had then the dray horses. This is one of the most pleasant memories of these days—marvellous—well groomed and decorated, well looked after and obviously loved by their drivers and everyone else.

I can (also) remember the brewery girls in the blue dresses and caps and wearing clog shoes.

The clogs use to clatter up the street. They became a sort of status symbol.

Apart from the larger industrial concerns the 'rag and bone and metal' merchant Asa Wass is still remembered with affection.

He had three pens, the main one being the office where Miss Wass, on receipt of the slip given by the Tallyman, after he had weighed the rags or whatever on a huge weighing machine, paid out the money. For one pound of woollens the price of tuppence was given.

In the third pen they had a huge metal cutting machine which made a constant tremendous racket. I suppose the people living in the tenements had no choice but to put up with it.

I'm sure the smell of the place still lingers in the nostrils of lots of local people.

Although Asa Wass' business was well known, one very rarely saw him or his wife Hannah. It was obviously a very lucrative business as can be seen of the property which both he and Hannah owned: No 161 Fountainbridge, comprising office, stables and yard, shops at 157, 159, 163a and 165a, seventeen houses at No 161 and a yard at 169. The houses were all rented out to local working people: a showman, labourer, charwoman, rubberworkers and millworkers.

Transport

Trams were very important to Tollcross, not least because it was a busy junction with its own depot, at least until the early 1960s.

They were good the trams. They were open at the driver's bit and they used to turn them. And quite often the kids used tae ask the tram driver if they could change the electric thing round for them. All they did was they put the seats back; the seats could go either way. The tram itself never turned round. You went upstairs and you walked the whole length of the car and then you opened this door and there was this little compartment there and the stairs went down to the driver. So we used to sit above the driver and drive him crazy! If you were making too much noise he would come up and sort you out.

There used to be a tram they called the Marchmont Circle and there used to be a conductor on it. And on his off duty days you used to see him and he was always dressed in plus fours. You would never have taken him for a tram conductor when he was off duty. And that man was on that route for donkey's years. There was quite a lot of characters—conductors—on the trams.

Tollcross was also close to Princes Street Station which was frequented by many who were not actually using the trains.

I used to love going to the Station to put money into the (chocolate) machine. Fry's had a machine. It was mostly stations where you got the machines. Occasionally a shop would have one outside and you could use it at night.

    When I started work I used to go down Lothian Road and cut through the goods yard into the Caley Station and out the other side to go down Queensferry Street. Sometimes they wouldn't let you through. There were three entrances (to the Station)—Lothian Road, beside the Caley Hotel and Rutland Street, plus the goods yard.

However, for local residents in the Morrison Street area the noise of the trains would have been difficult to live with.

Every night at 11.15 pm there was the sleeper train. And if you weren't in bed by 11.15 pm you had no chance of getting to sleep after it. But we got used to it. And then after the train had left they started gathering in a goods train. At

Fig 10.5: The West Port looking east from the Main Point. A long term employee describes the company of James Thomson, Motor Factors (shown in the picture) in this chapter.

night they gathered up the cars for the goods train for the morning run at
3.00 am. And they would take a whole train load of trucks, separate them,
shunt them onto another junction and give them a push, and there was a bang
with the wagons!

There was little road traffic until after the war. A man who worked for James
Thomson & Sons (later Thomson, Brown Ltd) Motor Factors of Lady Lawson
Street in 1919 recalls:

> We were the original earning folk in the motor world, right from the horses'
> days. When I started they sold whips, leggings, puttees and horses' collars. And
> then we kept the (car) spares for mainly the Ford and Morris cars. Cars—only
> toffs had them, with their chauffeurs. For petrol you had to go to a wee place
> in Morrison Street. There was no beautiful petrol pumps or showrooms. You
> got it in two gallon cans.
>
> I wanted to be a motor mechanic so I went to the Labour Exchange in
> Cambridge Street, but there were no jobs. They said, but here's a firm called
> James Thomson's, Motor Factors. Croalls was one of our big customers. They
> had a fleet of taxis, maybe 30 or 40, and they used to stand all along Castle
> Terrace, and they had green liveries.
>
> Most of the cars then were open and the driver had gloves, all muffled up.
> they had nae car heaters. We sold foot muffs for the lady passengers!

Entertainments

In Tollcross there was a whole variety of entertainments on the doorstep,
circus, theatre, cinema, indoor and outdoor bowls. There were also the street
entertainers such as Mrs Capaldi who came round with her barrel organ
pulled by a Shetland pony, and Willie Sives who played the spoons—also
sometimes at the Palladium.

> My mother liked the Palladium. It was just all different turns. You would have
> a comedian, a singer, somebody playing the accordian, and maybe a sketch or
> something. The Palladium used to have a show every night and twice on a
> Saturday. But a lot of people made it big down south from the Palladium. That's
> where they started off. So I think a lot of local people would probably go there
> rather than the King's. The King's Theatre was more classy, so it was different.
> More of the working class I suppose would favour the Palladium.

But it was the cinema which had the biggest audiences, and not just for the
films. It was a social occasion and if you were a couple you could opt for the
'Chummy Seats' in the back row where the snogging couples sat.

> It was in the King's Cinema (Cameo) they had the perfume machines. We used
> to go in there when we were teenagers. You put a penny and you pressed the
> button and stood in front of it. Ghastly perfume! Quite a few cinemas had them.
> One of us used to put it in and we'd all try and get it! It was great fun.
>
> There used to be a cinema in Lauriston Place called the Tollcross. It wis at
> the foot of ma stair. The Landlord we had then, he had sold out to the person
> who owned the cinema so I used to go into the cinema to pay the rent for the
> house. And if the landlord was feeling in a good humour he used to say 'just
> go in and see the picture'. So I used to get in for nothing.

Fig 10.6: Sean Connery, his wife Monique and George Brown, artist and contributor to this book. Mr Connery remembers Fountainbridge and Freer Street shown in the paintings behind. In his early working days he worked as a milkman with St Cuthbert's Cooperative, using such a milk cart.

It was great because you had your two films and then you had your trailer for the next week. And then you had a serial and cartoons. Serials just stopped. You used to have to go back the next week to find out what happened to the hero, you know, left hanging on a cliff or something!

It was quite nice when you went in. You entered from Lauriston Place and it had quite a big foyer. And I can remember one time getting in, and it must have been for a special matinee or something, an we got in wi' jam jars. Paid wi' jam jars. And I seem to remember we came out and got an orange and an apple or something. I can't remember why.

And then quite often the screen, you know, the thing, broke down and of course there used to be pandemonium, all the kids stamping their feet and shouting and whistling. Those days they used to take what they called buckies to the pictures; they had wee sorta snaily things inside them, I never liked them, but of course they used to take the shells and chuck them about in the dark because everything went black, you know. Because it always seemed to be at a good bit of the picture, or maybe the serial or something, it broke down.

Note

From recorded tapes featuring Ruth McLennan in conversation with Mrs M Main, Mrs M Grubb, Mr D Anderson, Mr Pinkerton, and Mr J McKenzie with additional material by Catherine Toall and Jean Redgers.

Appendix I

Williamson's Street Directory, Edinburgh & Leith 1786–88

Fountainbridge

Miss Arburthnot, Fountainbridge
William Bertram, wine merchant, Fountainbridge
Thomas Bishop, cornmonger, Fountainbridge
William Boggie, accomptant, Fountainbridge
Archibald Borthwick esq, Castlebarns
John Brown, wright, Fountainbridge
Thomas Calder, writer, Fountainbridge
Mrs Cameron, trunk maker, opposite Fountain Well
Colin Campbell, smith, Fountainbridge
William Caw, saddler, back of Fountain Well
Miss Clark, Fountainbridge
Mrs Clark, Fountainbridge
William Craw, saddler, back of Fountain Well
Alexander Cunningham, corn merchant, Fountainbridge
Misses Dargo, threed and mantuamakers, Fountain Close
Robert Dempster, apothecary, opposite Fountain Well
James Dewar, mason, Fountainbridge
Misses Dickson of Carberry, Fountain Close
Captain Durie, Fountainbridge
John Fernie, baker, Fountainbridge
Lady Forbes, Fountain Close
Alexander Gardner, of Exchequer, Fountainbridge
James Gardner, hairdresser, opposite Fountain Well
Mrs Gibson, Gardeners' Hall
Mrs Gellie, Gardeners' Hall
David Gordon, wright, opposite Fountain Well
John Guthrie, bookbinder, opposite Fountain Well
Mrs Hamilton, Fountainbridge
John Hodges, engraver, back of Fountain Well
George Imlach, writer, Fountainbridge Close
John Johnston, school master, Fountain Well
John Johnston, baker, Fountainbridge

Mrs Kennedy, Fountain Close
Alexander McDowgall, of Exchequer, Fountain Close
Thomas McGregor, baker, near the Fountain Well
Dr McKenzie, Fountainbridge
William McKenzie, back of Fountain Well
Mrs Morrison, midwife, Fountain Close
Lady Naesmith, Fountainbridge
Hugh Ormiston, grocer, Fountainbridge
Richard Ramsay, ladies hairdresser, opposite Fountain Well
William Robertson, broker, opposite Fountain Well
Lt Walter Ruddiman, Fountainbridge
Alexander Scott, brewer, Fountainbridge
Robert Semple, brewer, Castlebarns
Mrs Shiels, midwife, Fountainbridge
Mrs Stewart, room setter, Fountain Close
John Thomson, wright, Fountainbridge
William Tweedie, Fountain Close
Mr Vance, supervisor of excise, Castlebarns
Andrew Wauchope, turner, opposite Fountain Well
Mrs Westgate, Fountainbridge
William Wishet, trunk maker, back of Fountain Well
Anthony Wilkieson, gun smith, off Fountain Well
Mr Wood, Fountainbridge

Wright's Houses & Lochrin

John Aitken, shoemaker, Wright's Houses
James Archibald, innkeeper, Wright's Houses
Charles Cock, brewer, Drumdryan
Thomas Comb, clubmaker, Wright's Houses
Robert Currie, merchant, Burnsfield Links
Lady Dalrymple, Leven Lodge
Alexander Fraser, vinter, Wright's Houses
Bernard Henderson, starchmakers, Drumdryan
Haig Distillers, Lochrind (*sic*)
Thomas Lawson, starchmaker, Wright's Houses
Adam Luke, weaver, Wright's Houses
George Moffat, drover, Lochrind *(sic)*
George Morison, plasterer, Wright's Houses
David Ramsay, supervisor, Wright's Houses
John Richmond, weaver, Wright's Houses
Captain Rollow, Burnsfield Links

Lauriston

James Balmain, commissioner of excise, Lauriston
Revd Robert Bell, Lauriston
Andrew Bell, engraver, Lauriston
Miss Blair, Lauriston
John Borthwick, esq, of Crookston, Lauriston
Mrs Brown, Lauriston
James Brown, Lady Lawson's Wynd
Peter Crawford, late merchant, Lauriston
James Dunn, wright, Lauriston
Revd John Erskine, Lauriston
David Forbes, writer, Lauriston
James Forrest, writer to the signet, Lauriston
Robert Laurie, accomptant of excise, Lauriston
Captain Leslie, Lady Lawson's Wynd
Captain M'Donald, Lauriston
Colonel Riddel, Lauriston
Thomas Russel, wright, Lauriston
The Hon Lady Ruthven, dowager, Lauriston
Mrs Salton, Lauriston
Thomas Wharton, commissioner of excise, Lauriston

West Port

James Adie, shoemaker, West Port
James Arnot, baker, West Port
William Barrowman, leather merchant, West Port
John Brooks, baker, West Port
Robert Brown, leather merchant, West Port
John Cairns, Hay's Court, Main Point
Mrs Brown, cuttler, West Port
Wm Calder, grocer, West Port
James Carmichael, nailer, West Port
David Cleghorn, brewer, Kings Stables
George Combe, brewer, Livingston's Yard
Alexander Cunningham, shoemaker, West Port
Miss Dow, mantuamaker, Dallas's Land, West Port
Thomas Davie, tobacconist, West Port
James Duncan, baker, West Port
James Edie, shoemaker, West Port
Mrs Esplin, leather merchant, West Port
Hugh Ferguson, officer of excise, West Port
George Ferguson, West Port
Ebeneezer Gardner, linen manufactor, at the Cross, Workhouse West Port
    Vennel

Mrs Gardner, West Port, Vennel
Alexander Gardner, session clerk, West Kirk, head, West Port
William Gall, shoemaker, West Port
Mrs Gavin, rectifier, Main Point
Mrs Hamilton, candlemaker, West Port
John Hamilton, inspector of chimneys, West Port
Peter Hardie, brewer, West Port
Hugh Inglis, barber, West Port
Thomas Mair, clerk, to the friend. infur., West Port
John Neilson, shoemaker, Kings Stables, West Port
Captain Newlands, Hay's Court, Portsburgh
John Pettigrew, watchmaker, West Port
John Porteous, barber, without the West Port
Mrs Ramsay, Slunk
James Rain, spirit dealer, Main Point
John Reid, hairdresser, West Port
William Richardson, printers' inkmaker, King's Stables
Duncan Robertson, lint-dresser, West Port
James Ruddiman, hatter, a little without the West Port
James Ruthven, grocer, a little without the West Port; sells leather, and other
    shoemaker's articles
Robert Savage, shoemaker, West Port
John Scott, watchmaker, West Port
Mrs Sibbald, Slunk
Finlay Williamson, shoemaker, West Port

Appendix II

Three Hundred Years Of Weirs

Although the family of Weir is only one of many whose names appear regularly over the centuries in this region, they were more closely connected to Portsburgh, Lauriston and, in particular, to the lands of Tollcross. Unfortunately from the evidence so far it is not possible to say what relationship existed between them, if any, unless otherwise stated. The dates are taken from the Register of Sasines, the Register of Deeds, Minutes of the Town Council and other minor sources.

1605 *William Weir*, sheathmaker and son *Thomas Weir*, 'on the west side of the High Street of Portsburgh, on the south side of the Barras and north within the Dominion of Dalry, Barony of Inverleith, and Sheriffdom of Edinburgh.'

1623 *James Weir* (and his spouse Janet Wilsone), 'outwith the West Port.'

1649 *John Weir*, 'outwith the West Port' and brother of James Weir 1623.

1662 *Gabriel Weir*, merchant and Bailie of Edinburgh, 'of Dalry Milnes' and owner of the south croft of Tollcross (married to Susanna Lockhart). Son of *Gabriel Weir*.

1665 *Hew Weir*, Tailor, 'Portsburgh'.

1665 *James Weir*, Tanner, 'Portsburgh'.

1665 *Jean Weir*, 'Portsburgh', daughter of *William Weir*, tanner.

1669 *William Weir*, son of Gabriel Weir 1662.

1672 *Walter Weir*, merchant, 'of Dalry Milnes' and son of Gabriel Weir 1662, and owner of the south croft of Tollcross (married to Anne Johnstone).

1680 *Walter Weir*, merchant, brother of Gabriel Weir 1662.

1684 *Hugh Weir*, brewer, 'in Portsburgh'.

1686 *Hugh Weir*, tailor, 'Portsburgh'.

1722 *John Weir*, gardener, 'Heriot's Work' in Lauriston.

1726 *James Weir*, gardener and feuar 'Tollcross'.

1758 *James Weir*, wright and architect, 'Tollcross', son of James Weir, 1726. Born 1726 and died 1779.

1774 *James Weir*, armourer, 'on south side of the Kings Highway of Portsburgh'.

1781 *James Weir*, 58 Company in Royal Marines, later to become Major Weir, 'Tollcross', son of James Weir 1758 (married to Jean Stuart Ponton).

1820 *Thomas Graham Weir*, MD, *James Weir*, MD, of Tollcross and Drumsheugh, and sons of Major Weir 1781. T Graham Weir lived until
1895.

1849 *Isabella Weir* and husband Archibald Inglis MD, daughter of T G Weir
1820.

1898 *Jane Stuart, Margaret Graham, Janet Spens* and *Henry Alves Inglis*, all
grandchildren of *T G Weir* 1820.

Appendix III

The Lands Of Tollcross

Listed are the principal Superiors, Proprietors and Feuars (north and south crofts) where they are known. Dates from Registers of Sasines, Registers of Deeds, Minutes of Town Council and other minor sources.

1350 *Touris of Inverleith* (along with Dalry, High Riggs, Drumdryan, Orchard-field and Pocketslieve), north and south crofts.
1506 *Patrick Kincaid of that Ilk* (gives his whole lands of Tollcross to *John Campbell*.)
1601 *Barbara Scott*, Superior of lands of Tollcross.
1642 *Thomas Moodie* of Dalry, north and south croft.
1650 *Janet Moodie*, daughter of Thomas Moodie 1642, north and south croft.
1662 *Thomas Browne* (built mansion of Tollcross), north and south croft.
1662 *Gabriel Weir* of Dalry Milnes, merchant and Bailie of Edinburgh, south croft.
1679 *Walter Weir* of Dalry Milnes, merchant, son of Gabriel Weir 1662, south croft.
1704 *Town Council* buys land for 12 000 Merks from *Thomas Campbell*, flesher.
1715 *Agnes Campbell*, Lady Roseburn, Printress to Charles II, north croft.
1726 *William Carse*, wigmaker, north croft.
1726 *James Weir*, gardener, feuar, south croft.
1758 *James Weir*, architect, wright, south croft.
1782 *James Weir*, Royal Marines, south croft.
1782 *James Richmond*, nurseryman, north croft.
1790 *John Scott*, minister of Muthill (sons James, Colin and Peter), part of south croft.
1814 *Robert Wilson*, surgeon, north croft.
1814 *Alexander Young* WS, Superior, appears as Crown Vassal in report of Superiorities owned by Town (1816), north and south croft.
1818 *Alexander Scott*, lets land for Sheep and Cattle Market, the 'Bughts', part of south croft.
1818 *Elizabeth Wilson* (Mrs Chisholm of Chisholm), north croft.
1850 *T Graham Weir*, south croft.
1898 *Jane, Margaret, Janet & Henry Inglis*, south croft.

Index